VILLA DESIGN

VILLA DESIGN

AGATA TOROMANOFF

BRAUN

CONTENTS

Perlweiss
Architekten LEE + MIR

PREFACE

Originating as country residencies for nobility, villas have always been associated with generous, representative, and distinctive spaces. With styles evolving over the centuries and reflecting current trends or lifestyles, villas have remained a sophisticated and comfortable frame for everyday life. Today villa design has many names and faces, as architects push the boundaries using advanced technologies and materials. This book presents a range of over sixty examples of villas where the aesthetic and functional meet. Through various types and sizes, we look into contemporary interpretations of this traditional type of residential architecture. This book contains a great mélange of designs from all over the globe by both established architectural studios and emerging practices. Whether perched on a cliff or situated on the outskirts of a big city, the villas gathered here will delight architecture enthusiasts with their exciting structures and inventive spatial arrangements. Blending into their surroundings, many of them benefit from the combination of soothing natural landscapes and their proximity to an urban environment. The architects have envisioned villas that suit the owners' needs and tastes, from the pure and minimal to the monumental and extravagant. While some are inspired by organic shapes, other celebrate geometry. Thanks to the generous use of glass, all of them are spacious and filled with natural light, which enhances the unique modern forms. The use of transparency also initiates a fluent inside-outside relationship, which is crucial for all projects. Last but not least, as villas stand for a relaxed and luxurious lifestyle, the outdoor areas are particularly well thought out. Extensive and often equipped with a pool, they are connected with, and function as extensions of, the interiors.

Ursprünglich waren Villen Landsitze für den Adel; noch auch heute verbindet man mit ihnen die Vorstellung von geräumigen, repräsentativen und einzigartigen Gebäuden. Ihr Stil hat sich im Laufe der Jahrhunderte entwickelt und spiegelt die Tendenzen oder den Lebensstil ihrer Zeit wider; dennoch bieten Villen immer noch einen anspruchsvollen und komfortablen Rahmen für das tägliche Leben. Heutzutage werden Villen oft von einer Gruppe von Spezialisten entworfen, da die Architekten die Grenzen des Möglichen mit Hilfe der neuesten Technologie und Materialien überschreiten. Dieses Buch stellt eine Auswahl von mehr als sechzig Villen vor, die alle die Besonderheit haben, ästhetische Qualitäten mit großer Funktionalität zu verbinden. Über die Vielfalt der Typen und Dimensionen hinaus werden wir uns damit befassen, wie zeitgenössische Architekten diesen traditionellen Wohnungstyp interpretieren. Dieses Buch präsentiert eine große Anzahl von Projekten aus der ganzen Welt; die ausgewählten Villen sind das Werk sowohl etablierter als auch neuer Architekturbüros. Ob auf einer Klippe

Villa NEO
Querkopf Architekten

oder am Rande einer Großstadt gelegen, die hier versammelten Villen werden Architekturliebhaber mit ihren originellen Strukturen und innovativen Raumgestaltungen begeistern. Eingebettet in Naturlandschaften befinden sie sich gleichzeitig in der Nähe großer städtischer Zentren. Die Architekten haben sich Villen vorgestellt, die den Bedürfnissen und dem Geschmack der Eigentümer entsprechen, von einem reinen und minimalistischen Stil bis zu einem monumentalen und extravaganten Aussehen. Während einige von organischen Formen inspiriert sind, zelebrieren andere die Schönheit der Geometrie. Dank der großzügigen Verwendung von Glas und Öffnungen sind sie alle in natürliches Licht getaucht, was ihre einzigartigen, modernen Formen hervorhebt. Die häufige Verwendung verglaster Wände ermöglicht zudem eine fließende Beziehung zwischen innen und außen, die bei allen Projekten ein wesentliches Element darstellt. Nicht zuletzt sind die Villen ein Synonym für einen entspannten und luxuriösen Lebensstil; die Außenbereiche sind besonders gut gestaltet. Groß und oft mit einem Swimmingpool ausgestattet, bilden sie mit den Innenräumen, die sie vervollständigen und aufwerten, ein harmonisches Ganzes.

A l'origine, les villas étaient des résidences de campagne pour la noblesse ; de nos jours encore, l'idée de villa reste associée à celle d'édifices spacieux, représentatifs et singuliers. Leur style a évolué au fil des siècles et reflète les tendances ou le mode de vie de leur époque ; mais les villas offrent toujours un cadre sophistiqué et confortable pour la vie quotidienne. De nos jours, les villas sont souvent conçues par un groupe de spécialistes car les architectes repoussent les limites du possible en utilisant des technologies et des matériaux de pointe. Cette étude présente une palette de plus de soixante villas qui ont toutes pour particularité d'allier des qualités esthétiques à une grande fonctionnalité. Au-delà de la diversité des genres et des dimensions, nous nous intéresserons à la façon dont les architectes contemporains interprètent ce type traditionnel de résidence. Ce livre présente un grand nombre d'exemples du monde entier ; les villas sélectionnées sont l'œuvre tant de studios d'architectes établis que de nouveaux venus. Qu'elles soient perchées sur une falaise ou situées à la périphérie d'une grande ville, les villas rassemblées ici raviront les amateurs d'architecture par leurs structures originales et leurs aménagements spatiaux innovants. Ces villas, bien intégrées dans leur environnement, profitent de paysages naturels apaisants tout en restant à proximité de grands centres urbains. Les architectes ont imaginé des villas qui répondent aux besoins et aux goûts des propriétaires, d'un style épuré et minimaliste aux allures monumentales et extravagantes. Si certaines s'inspirent de formes organiques, d'autres célèbrent la géométrie. Grâce à une utilisation judicieuse du verre et des ouvertures, elles sont toutes baignées de lumière naturelle, ce qui met en valeur leurs formes modernes originales.
Le recours fréquent à de grandes baies vitrées permet également une relation fluide entre l'intérieur et l'extérieur, ce qui constitue un élément essentiel pour tous les projets. Enfin et surtout, les villas sont synonymes d'un style de vie détendu et luxueux ; les espaces extérieurs y sont particulièrement bien conçus. Vastes et souvent équipés d'une piscine, ils forment un ensemble harmonieux avec les intérieurs qu'ils complètent et agrémentent.

PENÍNSULA HOUSE

GUARUJÁ, SÃO PAULO, BRAZIL

This breathtaking location required equally spectacular architecture. Peninsula House is a weekend home located on the rocky São Paulo coast. The dramatism of the natural setting is enhanced by the unusual construction of the home, made of three volumes which are superimposed to minimalize the topographic impact. Another goal was to create a harmonic relationship between the inside and outside. The house is divided into three parts – the rectangular monolithic base and the triangular superior volume house private areas, while the transparent space connecting both is dedicated to common areas with an extensive pool terrace. The home theatre and four guest suites are located on the ground floor. The middle floor, at the heart of the house, is a meeting point and space for leisure. The top level with a master suite, which seems to be levitating in the air, offer two additional large and roofed balconies with panoramic vistas. One of the house's edges is a nine-meter cantilever towards the sea, to evoke the image of a large boat. The interiors are furnished with objects by famous Brazilian designers made of wood, which was also the material chosen for elements like the ceiling, panels, and joinery.

Dieser atemberaubende Ort verdiente ein ebenso spektakuläres Bauwerk. Das Península-Haus ist ein Wochenendhaus an der felsigen Küste von São Paulo. Die Pracht der natürlichen Umgebung wird durch die ungewöhnliche Form dieser dreistöckigen Villa verstärkt, deren Bauteile übereinander angeordnet sind, um die topografischen Einflüsse zu minimieren. Eine weitere Herausforderung war die Schaffung von Harmonie zwischen innen und außen . Das Haus ist in drei Teile gegliedert: Der rechteckige monolithische Sockel und das dreieckige Obergeschoss enthalten private Räume, während der transparente Zwischenbereich, der sie verbindet, den Gemeinschaftsräumen mit einer großen Terrasse mit Swimmingpool vorbehalten ist. Im Erdgeschoss befinden sich der Kinosaal und vier Gästesuiten. Das Zwischengeschoss im Herzen des Hauses ist ein Treffpunkt und bietet Raum für Freizeitaktivitäten. Im Obergeschoss, das in der Luft zu schweben scheint, befindet sich eine große Suite mit zwei überdachten Balkonen mit Panoramablick. Eine der Ecken des Hauses bildet einen neun Meter langen Ponton, der wie ein großer Ozeandampfer ins Meer ragt. Die Innenräume sind mit Holzobjekten ausgestattet, die von den besten brasilianischen Designern entworfen wurden. Holz ist auch das Material, das für Elemente wie die Decke, einige Wandverkleidungen und Tischlerarbeiten gewählt wurde.

Ce lieu à couper le souffle méritait une construction tout aussi spectaculaire. La Maison Península est une résidence de week-end située sur la côte rocheuse de São Paulo. La splendeur du cadre naturel est rehaussée par la forme inhabituelle de cette villa sur trois étages qui se superposent pour minimiser l'impact topographique. Créer une certaine harmonie entre l'intérieur et l'extérieur était un autre défi à relever. La maison est divisée en trois parties : la base monolithique rectangulaire et l'étage supérieur triangulaire abritent des espaces privés, tandis que l'étage transparent qui les relie est réservé aux pièces communes avec une vaste terrasse pour la piscine. La salle de cinéma et quatre suites pour les invités sont situées au rez-de-chaussée. L'étage intermédiaire, au cœur de la maison, est un point de rencontre et un espace dédié aux loisirs. L'étage supérieur qui abrite une grande suite, semble léviter dans l'air. Il est bordé par deux grands balcons couverts avec vue panoramique. L'un des angles de la maison forme un ponton de 9 mètres qui s'avance vers la mer comme s'il s'agissait d'un grand paquebot. Les intérieurs sont meublés d'objets en bois conçus par les meilleurs designers brésiliens. Le bois est aussi le matériau choisi pour des éléments tels que le plafond, certains panneaux et la menuiserie.

opposite:

Terrace view

Blick auf die Terrasse

Vue sur la terrasse

Exterior view Außenansicht Vue extérieure

ARCHITECTS: BERNARDES ARQUITETURA /// **COMPLETION:** 2017 /// **FURTHER PARTICIPANTS:** THIAGO BERNARDES, DANTE FURLAN, CAMILA TARIKI, FAUSTO SOMBRA, JOÃO FAIM, JOSÉ MIGUEL, MARCELO DONDO, ANA PAULA ENDO, ANTONIA BERNARDES, MARINA SALLES, MARIANA COHEN (ARCHITECTURE AND INTERIOR DESIGN TEAM) /// **FLOOR AREA :** 850 M² (9,150 FT²) /// **PHOTOS:** FERNANDO GUERRA

Exterior view Außenansicht Vue extérieure

Section

Schnitt

Section

Open-space living and dining area

Offener Wohn- und Essbereich

Salon et salle à manger en espace ouvert

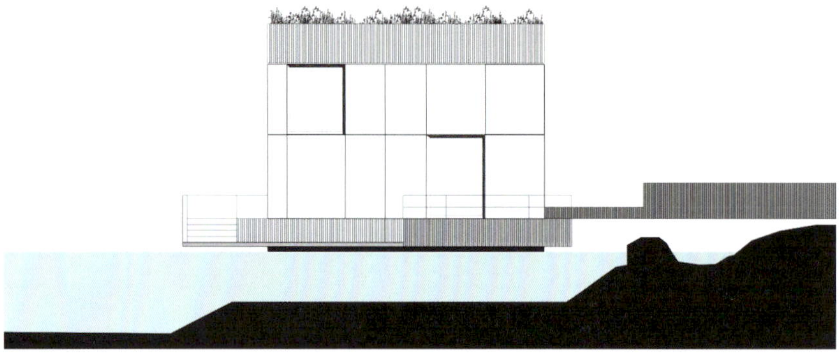

Exterior view

Außenansicht

Vue extérieure

ARCHITECTS: MECANOO /// **COMPLETION:** 2018 /// **FURTHER PARTICIPANTS:** ARQUITECTURA Y ORDENACIÓN URBANA S.L. AOU SL, BOHEME DEVELOPMENT S.L. /// **FLOOR AREA:** 600 M² (6,458 FT²) /// **PHOTOS:** MARIA SHOT

GLASS VILLA ON THE LAKE

LECHLADE, UNITED KINGDOM

The main goal for the architects was to design a house that would be both transparent and sustainable. Forging a strong relationship between the architecture and the lake landscape was at the core of the concept. Their aim to create harmony between the interior and the surrounding nature determined the selection of both materials and colours, as well as lighting. This is also why all of the villa's façades are fully glazed and offer uninterrupted views of the lake, sky, and forest, evoking the soothing feeling of living outdoors without compromising on the comfort of a house. The glass, offering a seamless connection between the architecture and nature, seems to make the building disappear. While entirely open to the natural context, the building is intimately hidden among dense trees and plants. Resembling a floating island, the house is connected on one side to the shore and on the other to the water surface, with terraces on two different levels. The energy consumption of the house was designed to be very low, using a variety of green technologies including an air thermal heat pump, solar panels, heat recovery systems, and triple glazed glass.

Das Hauptziel der Architekten war es, ein Haus zu entwerfen, das sowohl transparent als auch nachhaltig ist. Im Mittelpunkt des Konzepts stand die Beziehung zwischen der Architektur und Seenlandschaft. Die verwendeten Materialien und Farben sowie die Beleuchtung unterstreichen die Harmonie zwischen dem Inneren und der umgebenden Natur. In diesem Sinne sind auch alle Fassaden der Villa voll verglast und bieten einen Panoramablick auf den See, den Himmel und den Wald. Das gesamte Ensemble vermittelt das wohltuende Gefühl, unter freiem Himmel zu leben, ohne auf den Komfort eines Hauses zu verzichten. Durch den Einsatz von Glas verschwimmen die Grenzen zwischen Architektur und Natur, sodass das Gebäude scheinbar verschwindet. Obwohl es vollständig der umgebenden Natur ausgesetzt ist, wird es von Bäumen und Sträuchern verdeckt. Als ob sie auf dem Wasser stehen würde, ist die Villa über einen Steg vom Ufer aus zugänglich und ihre Silhouette spiegelt sich auf der Oberfläche des Sees. Sie ist mit zwei Terrassen auf verschiedenen Ebenen ausgestattet. Der Energieverbrauch des Hauses wurde dank des Einsatzes grüner Technologien, einschließlich einer Luftwärmepumpe, Solarzellen, Wärmerückgewinnungssystemen und Dreifachverglasung, so gering wie möglich gehalten.

L'objectif principal des architectes était de concevoir une maison qui serait à la fois transparente et durable. La relation entre l'architecture et le paysage lacustre était au cœur du concept : l'objectif était de souligner l'harmonie entre l'intérieur et la nature environnante. Cette quête d'harmonie a déterminé le choix des matériaux et des couleurs, ainsi que l'éclairage. C'est aussi dans cet esprit que toutes les façades de la villa sont entièrement vitrées et offrent une vue panoramique sur le lac, le ciel et la forêt. L'ensemble procure la sensation apaisante de vivre en plein air sans toutefois renoncer au confort d'une maison. Le verre, qui évite de créer une limite tangible entre l'architecture et la nature, semble faire disparaître le bâtiment. Bien qu'entièrement exposé à la nature environnante, le bâtiment est dissimulé par des arbres et des arbustes broussailleux. Comme si elle était posée sur l'eau, la villa est accessible par une passerelle depuis la rive et sa silhouette se reflète à la surface du lac. Elle est équipée de deux terrasses à des étages différents. La consommation d'énergie de la maison a été conçue pour être la plus faible possible grâce à l'utilisation de technologies vertes, notamment une pompe à chaleur thermique à air, des panneaux solaires, des systèmes de récupération de chaleur et du triple vitrage.

Interiors on the ground floor

Innenraum (Erdgeschoss)

Intérieur (rez-de-chaussée)

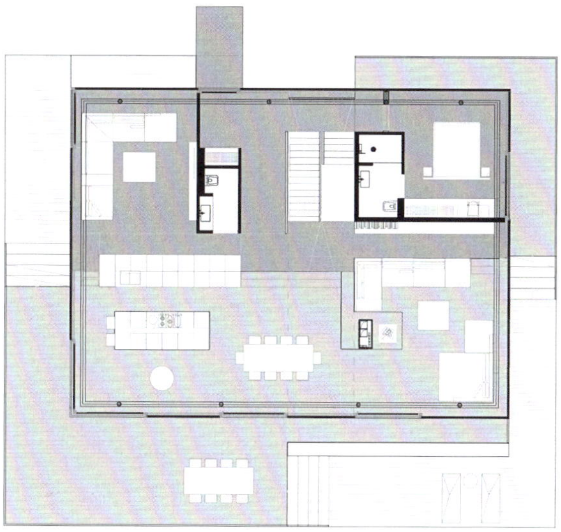

Staircase Escalier Treppe

Ground floor plan

Grundriss Erdgeschoss

Plan du rez-de-chaussée

QL HOUSE

ALGARVE, PORTUGAL

Built in a residential area on the Portuguese southern coast, the house stands out against the picturesque scenery of the Atlantic Ocean with its distinctive and bold volume. For the architects, this project was an exercise in balancing spaces and landscape integration with the ultimate goal of initiating a dialogue between the two. The intersection of two overlapping and perpendicular spaces creates a particular spatial dynamic and enhances the contrasting visual relations between full and empty, light and dark. The plan for this original two-storey building includes a living and dining room, a regular and a summer kitchen, four bedrooms, an office, a playroom, a sun room, and a swimming pool. An indoor garden with a continuous stairway along it provides a source of light and circulation. The living area is located in the glass cube and opens to a large outdoor leisure space around the pool. The roof of the living room acts as another terrace. The white concrete walls are designed for the warm climate, just as the numerous slats and motorised metallic shutters in the bedrooms filter excess sunlight without limiting the views of the surroundings.

Das in einer Wohnsiedlung an der Südküste Portugals errichtete Haus hebt sich durch sein kühnes und ungewöhnliches Erscheinungsbild von der malerischen Landschaft des Atlantischen Ozeans ab. Für die Architekten bestand die Aufgabe darin, ein Gleichgewicht zwischen den Formen des Gebäudes und ihrer Integration in die Landschaft zu finden. Ziel war es, einen kreativen Dialog zwischen beiden zu schaffen. Die Überschneidung zweier senkrecht aufeinander stehender Blöcke erzeugt eine besondere räumliche Dynamik und verstärkt den optischen Kontrast zwischen vollen und leeren Räumen sowie zwischen Licht und Dunkelheit. Dieses einzigartige Gebäude umfasst ein Wohn- und Esszimmer, eine Küche für den täglichen Gebrauch und eine für den Sommer, vier Schlafzimmer, ein Büro, ein Spielzimmer, ein Solarium und einen Swimmingpool. Ein Innengarten mit einer durchgehenden Treppe entlang des Gartens Sorgt für viel Licht und Luft. Die Wohnräume befinden sich im Glaskubus und öffnen sich zu einem großen Erholungsbereich im Freien rund um das Schwimmbad. Das Dach des Wohnzimmers dient als Terrasse. Dem warmen Klima entsprechend sind die Betonwände weiß gehalten und motorisierte Metalljalousien in den Schlafzimmern filtern das überschüssige Sonnenlicht, ohne die Sicht auf die Umgebung einzuschränken.

Construite dans un domaine résidentiel de la côte sud du Portugal, la maison se détache du paysage pittoresque de l'océan Atlantique par son allure audacieuse et insolite. Pour les architectes, l'exercice consistait à trouver un équilibre entre les formes du bâtiment et leur intégration dans le paysage. Le but était de susciter un dialogue créatif entre les deux. L'intersection de deux blocs juxtaposés perpendiculairement crée une dynamique spatiale particulière et renforce le contraste optique entre espaces pleins et vides, entre lumière et obscurité. Les plans de ce bâtiment original de deux étages comprennent un salon et une salle à manger, une cuisine des temps ordinaires et une cuisine d'été, quatre chambres à coucher, un bureau, une salle de jeux, un solarium et une piscine. Un jardin intérieur avec un escalier continu le long de celui-ci fournit une source de lumière et de circulation. Les pièces de séjour sont situées dans le cube en verre et s'ouvrent sur un grand espace de loisirs extérieur autour de la piscine. Le toit de la salle de séjour fait office de terrasse. Les murs en béton blanc sont conçus pour les climats chauds tout comme les nombreuses lattes et les volets métalliques motorisés des chambres à coucher qui filtrent l'excès de lumière solaire sans limiter la vue sur les environs.

ARCHITECTS: VISIOARQ - ARCHITECTS /// **COMPLETION:** 2016 /// **FLOOR AREA:** 1240 M² (13,347 FT²) /// **PHOTOS:** FERNANDO GUERRA | FG+SG

Exterior view Außenansicht Vue extérieure

Terrace view

Blick auf die Terrasse

Vue sur la terrasse

Exterior view Außenansicht Vue extérieure

CROWN HOUSE

FRANKFURT, GERMANY

Street façade

Fassade an der Straßenseite

Façade côté rue

Crown House is accessible from a small residential street. The street façade is geometrically designed and appears mostly closed. Its imposing size gives only an idea of how spacious the villa is, yet it is only after crossing the threshold that one realises the real scale. The welcoming two-storey hall is a great introduction to the living area, the library, and the home theatre, all interconnected on the ground floor. The hall also accommodates a wide staircase leading to the top level as well as to the dining area and the kitchen, which are located in the western part of the house. Upstairs, the architects arranged all the bedrooms and associated bathrooms around a gallery. The focal point here is the master bedroom, connected to a dressing room, a spa area, and a bathroom. Another attraction is the covered roof terrace offering panoramic vistas. Built in a hillside residential area in Frankfurt, Crown House benefits from stunning views of the valley. The southwest façade facing the garden is thus glazed from floor to ceiling. An extensive terrace and a pool on the ground level are complemented by big balconies on the upper floor, and by a garden designed by the same architects.

Das Crown Haus wird über eine kleine Wohnstraße erreicht. Die Straßenfassade zeigt sich geometrisch gestaltet und weitgehend geschlossen. Die imposante Fassade lässt die wahren Dimensionen der Villa kaum erahnen; erst nach dem Überschreiten der Eingangsschwelle erkennt man ihre innere Großzügigkeit. Eine einladende zweigeschossige Eingangshalle führt zum Wohnzimmer, zur Bibliothek und Heimkino, die sich in einem Teil des Erdgeschosses befinden und miteinander verbunden sind. Über die Eingangshalle erreicht man auch das Esszimmer und die Küche, die sich im westlichen Teil des Hauses befinden. Eine großzügige Treppe verbindet Halle und Obergeschoss. Im oberen Stockwerk haben die Architekten alle Schlafzimmer und angrenzenden Badezimmer um eine Galerie herum angeordnet. Das Hauptschlafzimmer, das mit einem Ankleidezimmer, einem Spa-Bereich und einem Badezimmer verbunden ist, steht im Mittelpunkt. Die überdachte Dachterrasse ist eine der Besonderheiten der Villa und bietet einen Panoramablick auf die Umgebung. Das an einem Hang errichtete Crown House bietet eine atemberaubende Aussicht über das Tal. Die Südwest-Seite mit Blick auf den Garten ist raumhoch verglast. Im Obergeschoss sind große Balkone vorgelagert, im Erdgeschoss gibt es ausgedehnte Terrassen mit einem Schwimmbecken, an die sich der ebenfalls von den Architekten gestaltete Garten anschließt.

On accède à Crown House par une petite rue résidentielle. La façade côté rue est marquée par des formes géométriques et en grande partie fermée. La taille imposante du bâtiment vu de l'extérieur ne donne qu'une faible idée de l'ampleur véritable de la villa ; ce n'est qu'après en avoir franchi le seuil qu'on se rend compte de sa superficie réelle. Un hall d'entrée accueillant de deux étages mène à la salle de séjour, à la bibliothèque et à la salle de cinéma, toutes situées au rez-de-chaussée et reliées entre elles. Le hall comprend également un large escalier menant à l'étage supérieur ainsi qu'à la salle à manger et à la cuisine qui sont situées dans la partie ouest de la maison. À l'étage, les architectes ont disposé toutes les chambres et les salles de bain annexes autour d'une galerie. La chambre principale, reliée à un dressing, un espace spa et une salle de bains en est le centre névralgique. La terrasse couverte sur le toit est l'une des particularités de la villa ; elle offre une vue panoramique des alentours. Construite dans un quartier résidentiel à flanc de colline à Francfort, la Crown House bénéficie d'une vue imprenable sur la vallée. La façade sud-ouest donnant sur le jardin est vitrée du sol au plafond. Des grands balcons à l'étage s'ajoutent à une vaste terrasse et une piscine au rez-de-chaussée qui sont prolongées par un jardin dont le tracé est signé des mêmes architectes.

ARCHITECTS: ALEXANDER BRENNER ARCHITEKTEN /// **COMPLETION:** 2018 /// **FLOOR AREA:** 650 M² (7,000 FT²) ///
PHOTOS: ZOOEY BRAUN

Façade opening up towards the garden

Fassade an der Gartenseite

Façade côté jardin

Terrace view

Blick auf die Terrasse

Vue sur la terrasse

Kitchen and dining area

Küche und Esszimmer

Cuisine et salle à manger

Entrance Eingangsbereich Entrée

SONNEN-BERG HOUSE

WIESBADEN, GERMANY

This horizontally stretched edifice is set in a picturesque landscape above the ruins of Sonnenberg Castle. The house sits at the rear of the plot, so one has to cross a small "piazza" with a visually hidden garage to reach the main entrance. Above it, a large empty space is the hub that is linked to all three floors. The striking lightness of the structure despite its significant scale was achieved thanks to floor-to-ceiling glass walls on most of the elevations. The ground floor is a fluid open space, leading from the hall to the living area with a fireplace, and further to the dining space and the kitchen. The upper levels are dedicated to private rooms, which all have balconies and loggias. To make it sustainable, the construction consists of aerated concrete as well as mineral and lime plaster. The house is heated by a geothermal heat pump, and electrical energy is provided by a large-scale photovoltaic system. The interiors, including all fittings and cabinet surfaces, have been custom made and designed by the architects as an integral part of the overall architecture.

Dieses horizontal gegliederte Gebäude liegt in einer malerischen Landschaft oberhalb der Ruine der Burg Sonnenberg. Das Haus befindet sich im rückwärtigen Teil des Grundstücks, sodass man den Eingang über eine kleine „Piazza" mit einer unsichtbar integrierten Garage erreicht. Über dem Haupteingang verbindet ein großer Luftraum alle drei Geschosse des Hauses miteinander. Die erstaunliche Leichtigkeit der Struktur ist trotz ihrer Größe den raumhohen Verglasungen auf der Aussichtsseite zu verdanken. Das Erdgeschoss ist ein fließender, offener Raum, der von der großen Eingangshalle in das Wohnzimmer mit dem Kamin und vom Esszimmer in die Küche führt. Das oberste Geschoss beherbergt die privaten Räume, die alle über Balkone oder Loggien verfügen. Die Struktur besteht aus Porenbeton mit einem Kalkputz-Auftrag, um eine nachhaltige Bauweise zu gewährleisten. Das Haus wird durch eine geothermische Wärmepumpe beheizt und der Strom wird durch eine Photovoltaikanlage erzeugt. Die Innenräume, insbesondere alle Einbauten und Schrankflächen, wurden von den Architekten im Rahmen einer ganzheitlichen Planung entworfen.

Ce bâtiment tout en longueur est placé dans un paysage pittoresque au-dessus des ruines du château de Sonnenberg. La maison se trouve à l'arrière du terrain, il faut donc traverser une petite «piazza» avec un garage dissimulé aux regards pour atteindre l'entrée principale. Au-dessus de celle-ci un grand espace vide donne accès aux trois étages. La légèreté étonnante de la structure en dépit de sa taille est due à des parois de verre qui courent du sol au plafond sur la plupart des murs. Le rez-de-chaussée est un espace ouvert fluide où l'on circule du grand hall au salon avec sa cheminée, puis de la salle à manger à la cuisine. Les étages supérieurs sont réservés aux pièces privées qui ont toutes un balcon et une loggia. Dans un souci de construction durable, la structure est composée de béton cellulaire et de plâtre minéral et calcaire. La maison est chauffée par une pompe à chaleur géothermique et l'énergie électrique est fournie par un système photovoltaïque. Les intérieurs et notamment tous les aménagements des chambres et les surfaces des armoires ont été réalisés sur mesure et conçus par les architectes comme partie intégrante du plan original.

Exterior view Außenansicht Vue extérieure

Entrance with the garage Eingangsbereich

Eingangsbereich mit Garage

Entrée avec garage

Pool Schwimmbad Piscine

ARCHITECTS: ALEXANDER BRENNER ARCHITEKTEN /// **COMPLETION:** 2017 /// **FLOOR AREA:** 575 M² (6,190 FT²) ///
PHOTOS: ZOOEY BRAUN

Kitchen and dining area

Küche und Esszimmer

Cuisine et salle à manger

Living room Wohnzimmer Salon

ARCHITECTS: DALUZ GONZALEZ ARCHITEKTEN /// **COMPLETION:** 2018 /// **FURTHER PARTICIPANTS:** POLIFORM ITALY /// **FLOOR AREA:** 500 M² (5,380 FT²) /// **PHOTOS:** VALENTIN JECK

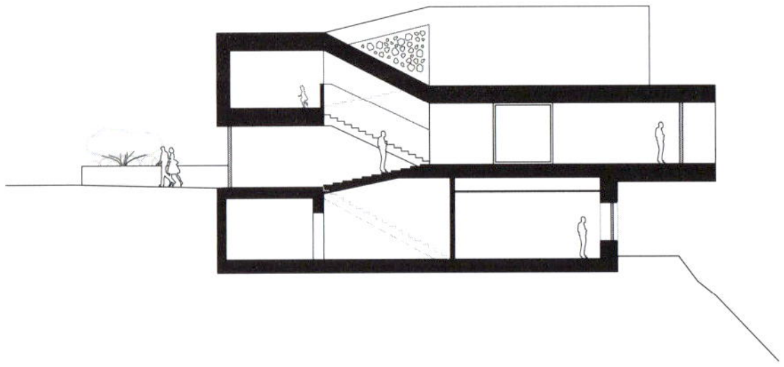

Section Schnitt Section

Exterior view Außenansicht Vue extérieure

Entrance Eingangsbereich Entrée

CASA MI

ZURICH, SWITZERLAND

This formidable construction of white superimposed volumes makes quite a statement on the right bank of Lake Zurich. Suspended over a steep slope, the purely geometric shapes emerge playfully out of one another to create a striking visual effect. Standing out from its natural surroundings, the colossus' main design was to open to the landscape. The gigantic panoramic windows in two shifted forms together with the terrace with an outdoor pool at the very end – making it appear as an extension of the lake – are not the only ways the structure benefits from the views. Thanks to a broadly scaled staircase connecting extensive open spaces, and also due to numerous openings in the side walls, often in original shapes responding to the angles of the walls, each space in the house offers a different perspective on the lake. Although the visual massiveness of the structure contrasts with the natural context, the spacious and well-lit interiors of the house are extremely well connected with the outside. At the same time, the architects made sure the shape evolves on all levels in a way that provides the inhabitants with maximum privacy.

Diese gigantische Konstruktion aus übereinanderliegenden weißen Blöcken ist eine Sensation am rechten Ufer des Zürichsees. An einem Steilhang aufgehängt, tauchen ihre rein geometrischen Formen spielerisch übereinander auf und bilden ein visuell markantes Ensemble. Obwohl sich das monumentale Gebäude deutlich von seiner natürlichen Umgebung abhebt, öffnet es sich dennoch, wie von den Architekten beabsichtigt, der Landschaft. Nicht nur die gigantischen Panoramafenster mit zwei versetzten Flügelfenstern und die Terrasse mit einem Außenschwimmbad am Hang – ein Pool, der den Eindruck erweckt, den See zu erweitern – verstärken den herrlichen Ausblick. Dank einer majestätischen Treppe, die weite offene Räume verbindet, und dank zahlreicher Fenster mit originellen Formen, die die Winkel der Seitenwände widerspiegeln, bietet jeder Raum des Hauses eine andere Sicht auf den See. Trotz der massiven Erscheinung des Bauwerks ist es leicht, von den geräumigen und gut beleuchteten Innenräumen nach außen zu gelangen. Gleichzeitig haben die Architekten dafür gesorgt, dass die Form auf jedem Stockwerk variiert, um den Bewohnern mehr Privatsphäre zu bieten.

Cette gigantesque construction de blocs blancs superposés fait sensation sur la rive droite du lac de Zurich. Suspendues sur une pente abrupte, leurs formes purement géométriques émergent de manière ludique les unes au-dessus des autres pour créer un ensemble visuellement saisissant. Bien que le bâtiment monumental se démarque nettement de son environnement naturel, il s'ouvre néanmoins, comme les architectes le souhaitaient, sur le paysage. Les gigantesques fenêtres panoramiques à deux battants décalés et la terrasse avec une piscine extérieure au bord de la colline - piscine qui donne l'impression de prolonger le lac - ne sont pas les seuls éléments qui mettent en valeur la vue panoramique. Grâce à un escalier majestueux qui relie de vastes espaces ouverts et grâce à de nombreuses fenêtres aux formes originales qui font écho aux angles des murs latéraux, chaque pièce de la maison offre un point de vue différent sur le lac. Malgré l'aspect massif de la structure, on passe aisément des intérieurs spacieux et bien éclairés aux parties extérieures. Dans le même temps, les architectes ont veillé à ce que la forme varie à chaque étage de manière à offrir aux habitants une plus grande intimité.

Pool Swimmingpool Piscine

Interiors Innenräume Intérieurs

Exterior view Außenansicht Vue extérieure

General view Gesamtansicht Vue générale

Section

Schnitt

Section

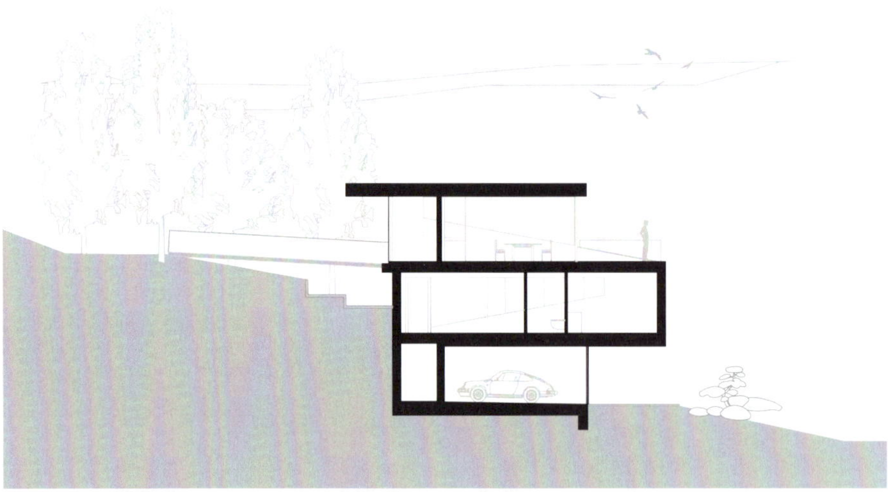

ARCHITECTS: ARCHITEKTEN LEE + MIR /// **COMPLETION:** 2016 /// **FLOOR AREA:** 360 M² (3,875 FT²) /// **PHOTOS:** DIRK WILHELMY

PERLWEISS

STUTTGART, GERMANY

The villa's dynamic volume seems to echo the hilly topography of its surroundings. Designed to meet their respective functions, three different polygons are superimposed and connected to each other by an asymmetrical façade. The overhangs of the different floors create covered outdoor spaces on the lower levels. The ground floor is decorated with silver panels with visible black joints in which three garage doors are concealed. The entrance to the building is located in the middle: it leads to a hall equipped with a cloakroom. From there, the first floor is accessed via a lift or a cantilevered stairway. The first floor consists of a study, a bedroom with bathroom and dressing room, a laundry room as well as a guest room with a separate entrance. The upper floor houses a spacious living room as well as a dining room with an open fireplace that serves as a decorative element but does not obstruct the view. As the kitchen is rarely used, it is hidden behind a wall of aluminium panels. The lift door as well as the access to the guest toilet and lighting are discreetly integrated into this furniture. The interior of marble, glass, metal and white surfaces is filled with natural light through a skylight above the stairwell that reaches down to the basement level. The roof terrace extends across the entire width of the house with a covered and heated area.

Der dynamische Charakter dieser Villa spiegelt die hügelige Topographie der Umgebung wider. Entsprechend der Nutzung sitzen drei unterschiedliche polygonale Grundrisse aufeinander und sind durch asymmetrische Fassadenflächen miteinander verbunden. Durch Hinausschieben einzelner Geschosse entstehen überdachte Außenbereiche. Das Sockelgeschoss wird durch silberne Fassadenplatten mit prägnanten schwarzen Fugen definiert, in der drei Garagentore unsichtbar integriert sind. In der Mitte befindet sich der Hauszugang, der zur Eingangshalle mit Garderobe führt. Von dort aus gelangt man mit dem Aufzug oder über eine frei auskragende Treppenstufe in das erste Obergeschoss. In diesem befindet sich der Arbeitsbereich, das Schlafzimmer mit Bad und Ankleide, der Hauswirtschaftsraum sowie ein Gastbereich, welcher über einen separaten Zugang verfügt. Im obersten Stockwerk befindet sich der großzügige Wohn- und Essbereich mit offenem Kamin, der als raumbildendes Element dient, jedoch Sichtbezüge nicht unterbricht. Da die Küche nur selten benutzt wird, ist sie hinter einer Verkleidung aus Aluminiumplatten verborgen. In dieses Einbaumöbel sind die Tür zum Aufzug sowie der Zugang zum Gäste-WC und die Beleuchtung unauffällig integriert. Der Innenraum aus Marmor, Glas, Metall und weißen Oberflächen wird durch ein Oberlicht über dem Treppenauge bis zum Sockelgeschoss mit natürlichem Licht gefüllt. Über die gesamte Hausbreite erstreckt sich die Dachterrasse mit einem überdachten und beheiztem Sitzplatz.

Le caractère dynamique de cette villa reflète la topographie vallonnée des environs. Dessinés pour répondre aux mieux à leurs fonctions respectives, trois polygones différents se superposent en désordre et sont reliés entre eux par une façade asymétrique. Les avancées dans le vide des différents étages créent des espaces extérieurs couverts en dessous. Le rez-de-chaussée est décoré de panneaux argentés avec des joints noirs apparents dans lesquels trois portes de garage sont dissimulées. L'entrée du bâtiment est située au milieu : elle mène à un hall équipé d'un vestiaire. De là, on accède au premier étage par un ascenseur ou par un escalier en saillie. Le premier étage comprend un bureau, une chambre avec salle de bain et dressing, une buanderie ainsi qu'une pièce réservée aux invités qui dispose d'une entrée séparée. L'étage supérieur abrite un séjour spacieux ainsi que la salle à manger avec une cheminée ouverte qui sert d'élément de décoration mais n'interrompt pas la vue. Comme la cuisine est rarement utilisée, elle est cachée derrière un lambris de panneaux d'aluminium. La porte de l'ascenseur ainsi que l'accès aux toilettes des invités et l'éclairage sont intégrés discrètement dans ce mobilier. L'intérieur de marbre, de verre, de métal et de surfaces blanches est rempli de lumière naturelle par une lucarne placée au-dessus de la cage d'escalier et qui plonge jusqu'au niveau du sous-sol. Le toit-terrasse s'étend sur toute la largeur de la maison avec un espace couvert et chauffé pour s'asseoir.

Staircase Treppe Escalier

Living space Wohnzimmer Salle de séjour

Kitchen and dining area

Küche und Esszimmer

Cuisine et salle à manger

Ground and first floor plans

Grundrisse Erdgeschoss und 1. Obergeschoss

Plans du rez-de-chaussée et du premier étage

VILLA HAUTERIVE

HAUTERIVE, SWITZERLAND

Occupying a site overlooking the lake of Neuchâtel and slopes with vineyards, Villa Hauterive was constructed over the basement of a pre-existing building. While the former underground level was redesigned and converted to function as a living space (which required that two small courtyards be dug into the topography on the east and west to bring natural light), the top volume takes the perimeter of the demolished structure and forms an entirely new single-storey space. Covered with a pure four-sided roof, it houses the living room with a massive bay window and glass façade that folds inwards to make a covered terrace, all to enjoy the panoramic views of the lake. The lower outdoor space was additionally equipped with a swimming pool. The architects selected an interesting mix of materials. While the bottom part is made of concrete and natural stone, the top volume is constructed from wood and glass. The interiors are arranged around the central staircase, linking both levels and topped with a skylight filtering natural light. The upper floor, envisioned as a fluid and aerial space, contrasts with the much more intimate lower level.

Die Villa Hauterive wurde auf den Fundamenten eines bereits existierenden Gebäudes auf einem Gelände mit Blick auf den Neuenburger See und die Weinberge errichtet. Während das ehemalige Untergeschoss umgestaltet und für die Unterbringung von Schlafzimmern umgebaut wurde (was die Einrichtung von zwei kleinen Höfen im Osten und Westen erforderte, um mehr natürliches Licht zu erhalten), nimmt das Obergeschoss den Umfang des abgerissenen Gebäudes auf und bildet einen völlig neuen eingeschossigen Raum. Von einem Walmdach bedeckt, beherbergt es ein Wohnzimmer mit einem großen Erker und einer weiteren Glasfassade, die sich nach innen klappen lässt, um eine überdachte Terrasse zu bilden, von der aus man den Panoramablick auf den See genießen kann. Im unteren Stockwerk wurde ein Außenpool eingerichtet. Die Architekten wählten einen originellen Materialmix. Während der untere Teil aus Beton und Naturstein besteht, ist das Obergeschoss aus Holz und Glas gebaut. Die Innenräume sind um ein zentrales Treppenhaus herum angeordnet, das die beiden Ebenen verbindet und von einem Oberlicht gekrönt wird, das das natürliche Licht filtert. Das Obergeschoss, das als fließender und luftiger Raum geplant ist, steht im Kontrast zu dem früheren Untergeschoss, das für mehr Privatheit sorgt.

Érigée sur un site surplombant le lac de Neuchâtel et des coteaux de vignes, la villa Hauterive a été construite sur les fondations d'un bâtiment préexistant. Alors que l'ancien sous-sol a été redessiné et transformé pour accueillir des chambres (ce qui a nécessité l'installation de deux petites cours creusées à l'est et à l'ouest pour procurer plus de lumière naturelle), l'étage supérieur reprend le périmètre de la structure démolie et forme un espace de plain-pied entièrement nouveau. Couvert d'un toit à quatre pans, il abrite une salle de séjour équipée d'une baie vitrée de grande dimension et d'une autre façade vitrée qui se replie vers l'intérieur pour former une terrasse couverte, le tout pour profiter de la vue panoramique sur le lac. Une piscine a été aménagée en extérieur à l'étage inférieur. Les architectes ont choisi un mélange original de matériaux. Alors que la partie inférieure est en béton et en pierre naturelle, l'étage supérieur est construit en bois et en verre. Les intérieurs sont disposés autour d'un escalier central reliant les deux niveaux et surmonté d'un puits de lumière filtrant la lumière naturelle. L'étage supérieur, envisagé comme un espace fluide et aérien, contraste avec l'ancien sous-sol beaucoup plus intime.

Exterior view Außenansicht Vue extérieure

ARCHITECTS: BAUZEIT ARCHITEKTEN /// **COMPLETION:** 2016 /// **FURTHER PARTICIPANTS:** GVH ST-BLAISE SA, ST-BLAISE (CIVIL ENGINEER), PRONA AG, BIEL-BIENNE (BUILDING PHYSICIST), GD RÉALISATIONS, NEUENBURG (SITE MANAGEMENT) /// **FLOOR AREA:** 638 M^2 (6,868 FT^2) /// **PHOTOS:** YVES ANDRÉ

Terrace view

Blick auf die Terrasse

Vue sur la terrasse

Interiors Innenräume Intérieurs

HOUSE R

VALVERDE, ITALY

Designed as a holiday home for a young couple, the house sits at the top of a slope. The geometric purity of the heavy cube punctured with square windows contrasts with its very unusual roof cover, which alludes to the site's topography. The roof's 45-degree rotation allowed the architects to create four identical trapezoidal sections. This solution has resulted in unified, yet complex interiors designed as a two-floor-high open space. The large living and dining areas, connected with a kitchen annex on the ground floor, and a mezzanine with two fully open bedrooms are conceived as one dynamic space, devoid of any structural elements inside. The windows in various sizes, placed irregularly on both levels, are juxtaposed with solid walls made of reinforced concrete. The numerous openings not only fill the house with light but also connect the interiors with the natural surroundings, including the large sliding door at the kitchen leading to an outdoor terrace. The landscape is beautifully framed by the large bedroom windows in particular. The dark grey, textured, and heat-reflective plaster covering all façades enhances the brutalist language, which is softened only with wooden elements like the window frames and doors.

Das als Ferienresidenz für ein junges Paar entworfene Haus liegt am oberen Ende eines Hanges. Die geometrische Reinheit dieses massiven, von quadratischen Fenstern durchbrochenen Kubus steht im Kontrast zu der sehr ungewöhnlichen Form des Daches, die deutlich auf die Topographie des Ortes anspielt. Durch die Absenkung des Daches um 45 Grad konnten die Architekten vier identische, trapezförmige Abschnitte schaffen. Diese Unterteilung hat den Vorteil, dass sie einen einheitlichen, jedoch auch aufwändigen Innenbereich bietet, der einen offenen Raum auf zwei Etagen bildet. Das große Wohnzimmer, das durch eine Küche mit dem Esszimmer im Erdgeschoss verbunden ist, und das Zwischengeschoss mit zwei offenen Schlafzimmern sind als ein einzigartiger und dynamischer Raum ohne jegliche innere Bauteile gestaltet. Die unterschiedlich großen Fenster, die unregelmäßig auf beiden Ebenen platziert sind, stehen neben massiven Stahlbetonwänden. Diese zahlreichen Lichtöffnungen bringen nicht nur Licht in das Herz des Hauses, sondern verbinden auch den Innenraum mit der umgebenden Natur; die große Schiebetür in der Küche führt beispielsweise zu einer Außenterrasse. Große Schlafzimmerfenster geben den Blick auf die Landschaft frei. Der dunkelgraue, strukturierte, wärmereflektierende Putz, der alle Fassaden bedeckt, unterstreicht die brutalistische Formensprache, die nur durch einige wenige Holzelemente wie Fensterrahmen und Türen gedämpft wird.

Conçue comme une résidence de vacances pour un jeune couple, la maison se trouve au sommet d'une pente. La pureté géométrique de ce cube massif percé de fenêtres carrées contraste avec la forme très inhabituelle de la toiture qui fait clairement allusion à la topographie du site. Le basculement de la toiture de 45 degrés a permis aux architectes de créer quatre sections trapézoïdales identiques. Cette division a l'avantage d'offrir des volumes tout à la fois complexes et unis qui forment un espace ouvert sur deux étages. La grande salle de séjour et la salle à manger, reliées par une cuisine au rez-de-chaussée, et la mezzanine avec deux chambres à coucher entièrement ouvertes sont conçues comme un espace unique et dynamique dépourvu de tout élément structurel intérieur. Les fenêtres de taille variable, placées de façon irrégulière sur les deux niveaux, sont juxtaposées à des murs solides en béton armé. Ces ouvertures nombreuses apportent non seulement de la lumière au cœur de la maison ; elles relient aussi l'intérieur à la nature environnante ; la grande porte coulissante de la cuisine mène par exemple à une terrasse extérieure. Le paysage est magnifiquement mis en valeur par les grandes fenêtres des chambres. Le plâtre gris foncé, texturé et réfléchissant la chaleur qui recouvre toutes les façades donne une touche brutaliste qui n'est atténuée que par quelques éléments en bois comme les cadres de fenêtres et les portes.

ARCHITECTS: 35A STUDIO /// **COMPLETION:** 2017 /// **FURTHER PARTICIPANTS:** ANDREA CARMIGNOLA ARCHITETTO, JANKO MAURI /// **FLOOR AREA:** 120 M² (1,292 FT²)/// **PHOTOS:** ANDREA CARMIGNOLA ARCHITETTO, MADDALENA MERLO ARCHITETTO

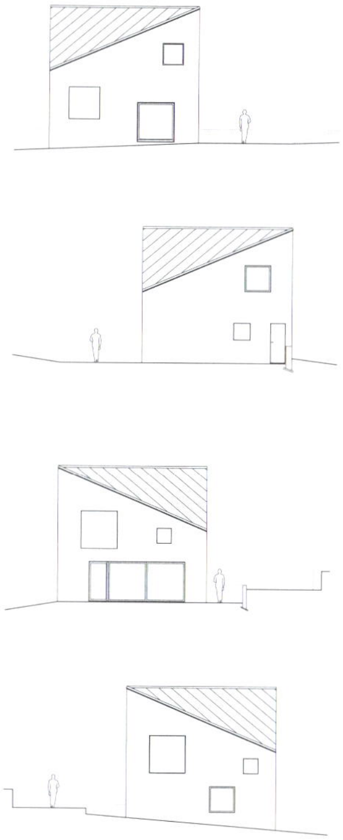

Exterior view Außenansicht Vue extérieure

Section

Schnitt

Section

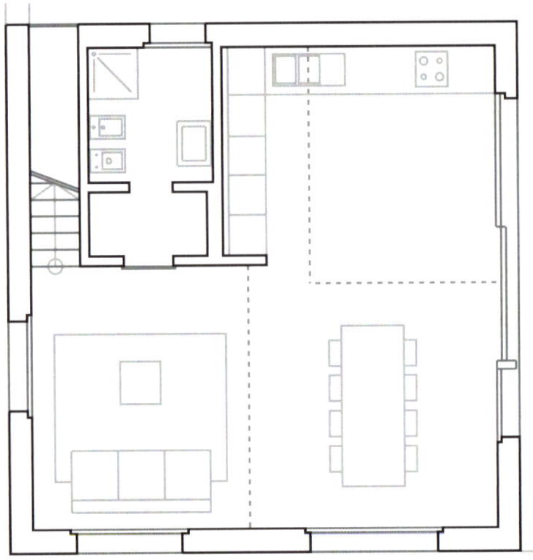

Living and dining area

Wohn- und Esszimmer

Salon et salle à manger

Ground floor plan

Grundriss Erdgeschoss

Plan du rez-de-chaussée

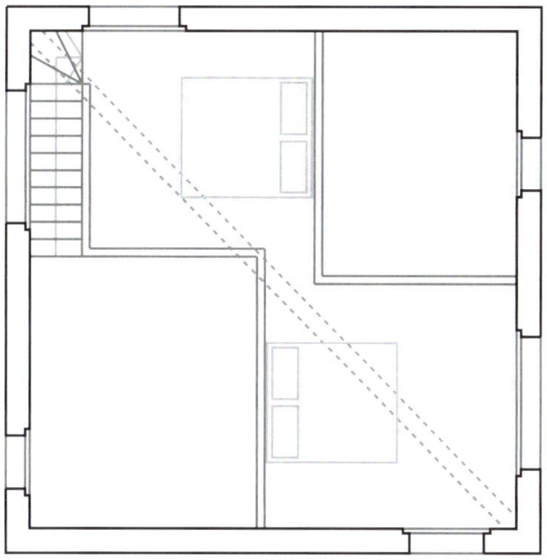

Mezzanine plan

Grundriss Zwischengeschoss

Plan du mezzanine

Mezzanine Zwischengeschoss Mezzanine

Exterior view Außenansicht Vue extérieure

ARCHITECTS: BENJAMIN HELLER /// **COMPLETION:** 2017 /// **FLOOR AREA:** 183 M² (1,970 FT²) /// **PHOTOS:** BENJAMIN HELLER

BLACK HOUSE

ÖHNINGEN, GERMANY

Set in an idyllic health resort at Lake Constance in Germany, Black House is located on the outskirts of the village, which lies along the national border with Switzerland. The visually striking, dark volume resembles a multifaceted stone with its various angles, polygonal shapes, large openings, and suspended façade. The house looks different depending on one's perspective, an effect which is enhanced by the play of light and shadows on its curved surfaces. The space is divided into public rooms on the lower floor and private ones on the upper level. The different size of the rooms additionally indicate their character. Clear, simple forms and restrained colours are the main features of the interior design, all not to divert the attention from the extraordinary views one can enjoy through the huge windows on both floors, as the house is directed towards the landscape and the water. The inside and outside are well connected despite the massive structure. The solid construction of Black House is made of wood. A heat pump connected with a ground heat collector makes the house energetically autonomous.

Das Schwarze Haus liegt in einem idyllischen Kurort am Bodensee, am Rande eines Dorfes nahe der Schweizer Grenze. Die dunkle, auffällige Masse des Gebäudes gleicht einem facettenreichen Stein mit seinen Kanten, den polygonalen Formen, den großen Fenstern und der vorgehängten Fassade. Das Erscheinungsbild des Hauses ist je nach Blickwinkel unterschiedlich, vor allem durch das Licht- und Schattenspiel auf seinen geknickten Oberflächen. Das Gebäude ist unterteilt in öffentlich oder halböffentlich genutzte Räume im unteren Stockwerk und private Räume im oberen Stockwerk. Die unterschiedliche Höhe und Größe der Räume zeigt intuitiv ihre jeweilige Funktion an. Die Inneneinrichtung wird von einfachen und klaren Formen und schlichten Farben dominiert, um die Aufmerksamkeit nicht von dem außergewöhnlichen Panorama abzulenken, das man durch die großen Fenster auf beiden Etagen genießen kann. Innen und außen sind trotz der massiven Struktur gut miteinander verbunden. Die massive Konstruktion von Black House besteht aus Holz. Eine Wärmepumpe, die mit einem Erdwärmekollektor verbunden ist, macht das Haus energetisch unabhängig.

Située dans une station thermale idyllique au bord du lac de Constance en Allemagne, la Maison Noire se trouve à la périphérie du village près de la frontière suisse. La masse sombre de l'édifice, qui attire les regards, ressemble à une pierre aux multiples facettes avec ses arêtes, ses formes polygonales, ses grandes ouvertures et sa façade suspendue. L'aspect de la maison diffère selon le point de vue, d'autant plus que la lumière et l'ombre jouent sur ses surfaces courbes. L'espace est divisé en pièces d'usage public ou semi-public à l'étage inférieur et en chambres privées à l'étage supérieur. La hauteur et la taille variables des pièces indiquent intuitivement leurs fonctions respectives. La décoration intérieure est dominée par des formes simples et claires et des couleurs sobres pour ne pas détourner l'attention du panorama extraordinaire dont on peut profiter à travers les grandes fenêtres qui équipent les deux étages, car la maison est toute tournée vers le paysage et le lac. Malgré sa structure massive, on passe facilement de l'intérieur à l'extérieur de la maison. L'ossature de la Maison Noire est en bois. Une pompe à chaleur reliée à un collecteur de chaleur au sol la rend énergétiquement autonome.

Staircase Treppe Escalier

Interiors on the first floor

Innenraum (Obergeschoss)

Intérieur (premier étage)

Ground and first floor plans

Grundriss Erd- und Obergeschoss

Plans du rez-de-chaussée et du premier étage

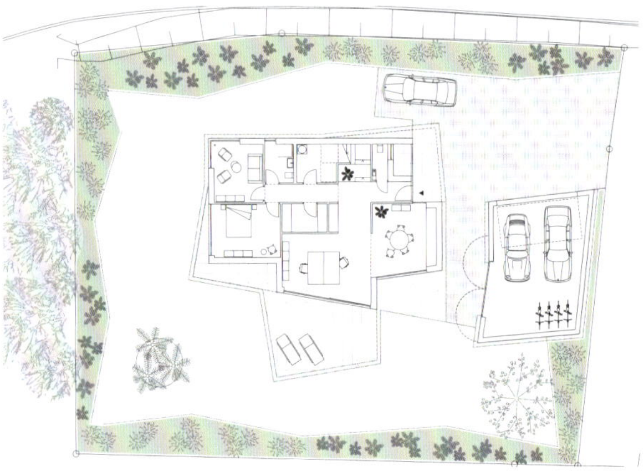

Façade opening up towards the garden

Fassade an der Gartenseite

Façade côté jardin

VILLA L

COLOGNE, GERMANY

Villa L embodies the timeless beauty of pure geometry. The architect's main goal was to design a structure that would highlight the picturesque views to the east and to the west. Another challenge was the owner's wish to create a garden facing the south. As a result, the house was based on a traditional longhouse model with two floors. This simplified form nevertheless has contemporary touches, like extensive openings on both levels, and surfaces cut out of the basic shape. All façades are planned differently, adjusted not only to the outside perspective but also to the function of particular spaces inside the house. The grassy garden area is connected to the house with a large outdoor seating terrace. The clarity of forms and the linear order also dominate in the interiors. The white surfaces of the walls and ceilings are complemented by wooden floors and finishing elements, like the stairs and the wide seats in the stunning bay windows. Similarly, the street side façade on the ground level is mostly covered with greywacke, which contrasts with the white walls.

Die Villa L ist eine Hommage an die zeitlose Schönheit reiner geometrischer Formen. Das Hauptziel des Architekten war es, eine Struktur zu entwerfen, die die malerische Aussicht auf den Osten und Westen des Hauses unterstreicht. Der Eigentümer seinerseits wollte einen nach Süden ausgerichteten Garten anlegen. Daher wurde das Haus nach einem traditionellen zweistöckigen Langhausmodell gebaut. Diese vereinfachte Struktur weist jedoch kleine zeitgenössische Akzente auf, wie zum Beispiel große Fenster in beiden Stockwerken und Einschnitte in der rechteckigen Struktur. Alle Fassaden sind unterschiedlich gestaltet und nicht nur an die Außenperspektive, sondern auch an die Funktion der Räume, denen sie im Inneren des Hauses zugewandt sind, angepasst. Der Rasengarten ist durch einen großen Außensitzbereich mit dem Haus verbunden. Auch in der Innenarchitektur dominieren Formenreinheit und lineare Ordnung. Die weißen Flächen der Wände und Decken sind durch Parkettböden und Holzelemente passend ergänzt, ebenso wie die Treppen und die breiten Sitze, die die prächtigen Erkerfenster zieren. Die straßenseitige Fassade im Erdgeschoss ist mit Grauwacke verkleidet, die einen Kontrast zu den weißen Wänden bildet.

La Villa L rend hommage à la beauté intemporelle des formes géométriques pures. L'objectif principal de l'architecte était de concevoir une structure qui mettrait en valeur les vues pittoresques à l'est et à l'ouest de la maison. De son côté, le propriétaire souhaitait créer un jardin orienté vers le sud. En conséquence, la maison a été construite sur un modèle assez traditionnel de maison longue à deux étages. Cette structure simple intègre néanmoins des petites touches contemporaines, comme de grandes ouvertures sur les deux étages et des incisions dans la structure rectangulaire. Toutes les façades sont conçues différemment et adaptées non seulement à la perspective extérieure mais également à la fonction des pièces sur lesquelles elles donnent à l'intérieur de la maison. Le jardin planté de gazon est relié à la maison par un grand espace extérieur. La pureté des formes et l'ordre linéaire dominent également dans la décoration intérieure. Les surfaces blanches des murs et des plafonds sont agrémentées de parquets et d'éléments de finition en bois, tout comme les escaliers et les larges sièges qui ornent les splendides baies vitrées. La façade côté rue, au rez-de-chaussée, est recouverte de grauwacke, ce qui forme un contraste avec les murs blancs.

Street façade

Fassade an der Straßenseite

Façade côté rue

ARCHITECTS: BENJAMIN VON PIDOLL ARCHITEKTUR /// **COMPLETION:** 2016 /// **FLOOR AREA:** 290 M^2 (3,120 FT^2) ///
PHOTOS : PHILIP KISTNER

Façade opening up towards the garden

Fassade an der Gartenseite

Façade côté jardin

Exterior view Außenansicht Vue extérieure

ORIGAMI HOUSE

PORTO FELIZ, SÃO PAULO, BRAZIL

Exterior view Außenansicht Vue extérieure

Built 50 minutes away from São Paulo, Origami House is the main residence of a couple. The building was designed in harmony with the topography, while solutions for isolation and ventilation respond to the local natural conditions. Its owners' main wish was a single-storey structure, practical for everyday life. As they are frequently visited by their children and grandchildren, the house also had to be spacious, with a focus on social spaces. In response, the architects planned three bedrooms, a comfortable home office, a kitchen, and a living area on the ground floor. Additionally, three guest rooms occupy the lower level. The most unique feature of the space arrangement is the connection between the living room and the terrace with a pool. The large glass windows are easily removable, so both spaces are fluidly integrated. Concrete is the dominating material used in the common areas, where it contrasts with wooden furniture. It also protects the west façade of the house from the afternoon sun. The private space of the house is located in a perpendicular metallic pavilion, with façades rhythmically protected by wooden brise-soleils.

Die Villa Origami, 50 Autominuten von São Paulo entfernt, ist der Hauptwohnsitz eines Ehepaares. Das Gebäude wurde mit Rücksicht auf die umgebende Topografie entworfen. Auch die Isolierungs- und Belüftungslösungen sind an die örtlichen natürlichen Gegebenheiten angepasst. Die Eigentümer wünschten sich ein einstöckiges, alltagstaugliches Haus mit ausreichend Platz für gesellige Zusammenkünfte und ihre Enkelkinder, die sie regelmäßig besuchen. Die Architekten schufen daher drei Schlafzimmer, ein komfortables Arbeitszimmer sowie eine Küche und ein Wohnzimmer im Erdgeschoss. Im Untergeschoss befinden sich drei Gästezimmer. Das Ensemble, das aus dem Wohnzimmer und der Terrasse mit Swimmingpool besteht, ist das charakteristischste Merkmal der Raumaufteilung. Die großen Glasfenster sind leicht abnehmbar, sodass die beiden Räume nahtlos ineinander übergehen. Beton ist das dominierende Material in den Gemeinschaftsräumen, wo es einen schönen Kontrast zu den Holzmöbeln bildet. Er schützt auch die Westfassade des Hauses vor der Nachmittagssonne. Die privaten Räume des Hauses befinden sich in einem rechteckig geformten Pavillon aus Metall, dessen Fassade von in regelmäßigen Abständen platzierten, hölzernen Brise Soleils geschützt wird.

Construite à 50 minutes en voiture de São Paulo, la villa Origami est la résidence principale d'un couple. Le bâtiment a été conçu dans le respect de la topographie environnantes, tandis que les solutions d'isolation et de ventilation sont adaptées aux conditions naturelles locales. Le souhait des propriétaires de la villa était d'avoir une maison d'un seul étage et pratique pour la vie quotidienne. Comme ils reçoivent régulièrement la visite de leurs enfants et petits-enfants, la villa devait être suffisamment spacieuse et les pièces communes ont été privilégiées. Les architectes ont donc créé trois chambres à coucher, un bureau confortable, ainsi qu'une cuisine et un salon au rez-de-chaussée. Trois chambres d'hôtes occupent le sous-sol. L'ensemble formé par le salon et la terrasse avec piscine est la caractéristique la plus emblématique de l'aménagement de l'espace. Les grandes fenêtres en verre sont facilement amovibles, de sorte que les deux espaces sont intégrés de manière fluide. Le béton est le matériau dominant dans les espaces communs où il forme un joli contraste avec le mobilier en bois. Il protège également la façade ouest de la maison du soleil de l'après-midi. L'espace privé de la maison est situé dans un pavillon métallique perpendiculaire dont les côtés sont protégés à intervalles réguliers par des brise-soleil en bois.

ARCHITECTS: BERNARDES ARQUITETURA /// **COMPLETION:** 2017 /// **FURTHER PARTICIPANTS:** THIAGO BERNARDES, DANTE FURLAN, CAMILA TARIKI, ANTONIA BERNARDES, BRUNO MILAN, PÉROLA MACHADO (TEAM ARCHITECTURE AND INTERIOR DESIGN) /// **FLOOR AREA:** 670 M² (7,210 FT²) /// **PHOTOS:** LEONARDO FINOTTI

Pool Swimmingpool Piscine

Terrace view

Blick auf die Terrasse

Vue sur la terrasse

Entrance Eingangsbereich Entrée

Pool Swimmingpool Piscine

Façade opening up towards the garden

Façade côté jardin

Fassade an der Gartenseite

Living space Wohnzimmer Salle de séjour

AGLAE HOUSE

SANTO DOMINGO, VALPARAISO, CHILE

The design of this weekend house in coastal Santo Domingo, located 120 kilometres (75 miles) from Santiago, Chile, is adjusted to the local weather conditions. As the site is exposed to strong winds, particularly from the west in the summer, the architects decided to build the house in parallel to the length of the land, in the east-west direction. This created a protected interior courtyard facing the living area, with wall-to-ceiling windows that smoothly connect the indoor and outdoor areas when opened. To reinforce the cosy atmosphere, the terrace with a small pool is closed towards the street by a wooden wall covered with slats of larch wood in different lengths. All windows in the house are planned to face the north to maximise the access of sunlight, with one exception: the master bedroom window looks towards the west to enjoy views of the sunset. In contrast, the south elevation with the entrance is protectively devoid of openings. The simplified construction of this single-storey house is expressed with pure geometry. Based on pine pillars with iron slab and partition walls, its exterior façades are coated in impregnated pine wood.

Die Architektur dieses Wochenendhauses an der Küste von Santo Domingo, 120 Kilometer von Santiago entfernt, ist an die Wetterbedingungen des Ortes angepasst. Da das Gelände starken Winden ausgesetzt ist, insbesondere denen, die im Sommer von West nach Ost wehen, beschlossen die Architekten, das Haus in Ost-West-Richtung und entlang der gesamten Grundstückfläche zu bauen. Durch diese Ausrichtung entstand unmittelbar vor dem Wohnbereich ein windgeschützter Innenhof mit raumhohen Fenstern, die im geöffneten Zustand innen und außen nahtlos miteinander verbinden. Für mehr Ruhe ist die Terrasse mit einem kleinen Swimmingpool durch eine Holzwand von der Straße getrennt, die aus unterschiedlich langen Lärchenholzlatten besteht. Alle Fenster des Hauses sind nach Norden ausgerichtet, um den Zugang zu natürlichem Licht zu maximieren, mit einer Ausnahme: Das Fenster des Hauptschlafzimmers ist nach Westen ausgerichtet, um den Blick auf den Sonnenuntergang zu genießen. An der Südfassade, wo sich der Haupteingang befindet, gibt es keine Fenster. Der Eindruck von Leichtigkeit, den dieses einstöckige Haus vermittelt, ist auf seine reinen geometrischen Formen zurückzuführen. Die Basis bildet ein Kiefernsockel mit Eisenplatten und -trennwänden, die Aussenfassaden sind mit imprägnierten Kiefernlamellen verkleidet.

L'architecture de cette maison de week-end sur la côte de Santo Domingo, à 120 kilomètres de Santiago, est adaptée aux conditions météorologiques du lieu. Comme le site est exposé à des vents violents, en particulier ceux soufflant d'ouest en est durant l'été, les architectes ont décidé de construire la maison dans la direction est-ouest et dans le sens de la longueur du terrain. Cette orientation a permis de créer une cour intérieure protégée des vents juste devant la zone d'habitation, avec des fenêtres qui vont du mur au plafond et forment un point de passage entre l'intérieur et l'extérieur lorsqu'elles sont ouvertes. Pour plus d'intimité, la terrasse avec une petite piscine est séparée de la rue par un mur en bois recouvert de lattes de mélèze de différentes longueurs. Toutes les fenêtres de la maison sont orientées vers le nord afin de maximiser l'accès à la lumière naturelle, à une exception près : la fenêtre de la chambre à coucher principale donne sur l'ouest pour profiter de la vue sur le coucher du soleil. En revanche, la façade sud où se trouve l'entrée est dépourvue d'ouvertures. L'impression de légèreté que donne cette maison de plain-pied est due à ses formes géométriques épurées. Elle est bâtie sur un socle en pin qui soutient une dalle en fer et des cloisons de séparation. Ses façades extérieures sont revêtues de lattes de pin imprégné.

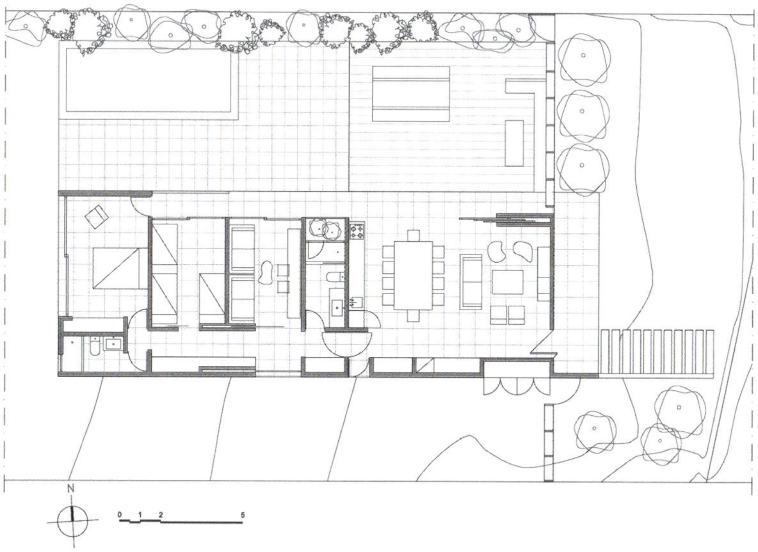

North view Blick von Norden Vue du nord

Main floor plan

Gesamtplan

Plan d'ensemble

ARCHITECTS: ANDRÉS FARÍAS - AFARQ /// **COMPLETION:** 2018 /// **FLOOR AREA:** 140 M² (1,500 FT²) /// **PHOTOS:** PABLO BLANCO

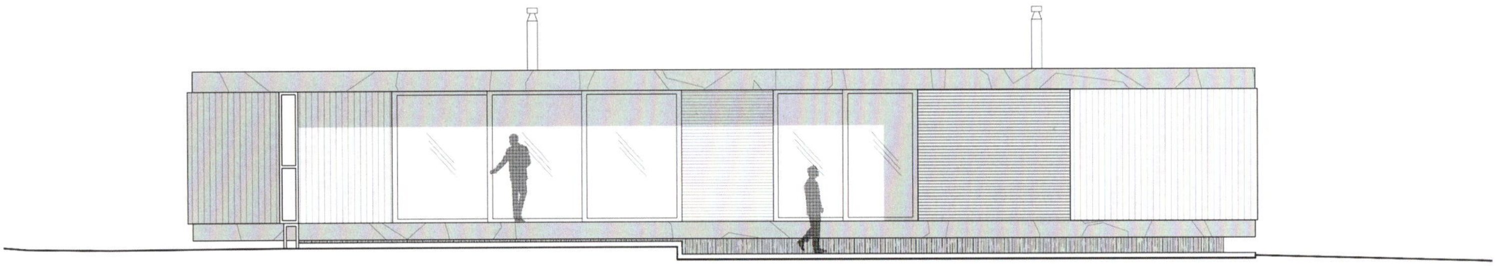

Section Schnitt Section

South view Blick von Süden Vue du sud

ARCHITECTS: BIEHLER WEITH - BUILDING DESIGN PROJECTS /// **COMPLETION:** 2018 /// **FLOOR AREA:** 375 M^2 (4,040 FT^2) /// **PHOTOS:** BRIGIDA GONZÁLEZ

Section Schnitt Section

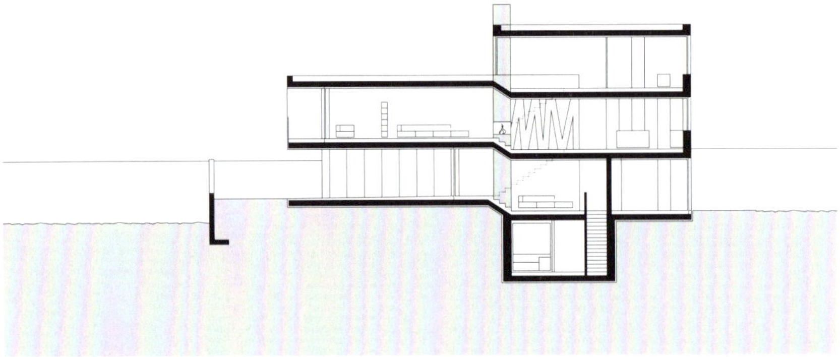

Façade opening up towards the garden

Fassade an der Gartenseite

Façade côté jardin

Street façade

Fassade an der Straßenseite

Façade côté rue

SONNEN-HANG

ABTWIL, SWITZERLAND

The entrance façade on the street level may be misleading. It consists of three solid volumes on two levels, devoid of any openings except for the main door, which seems to contradict the multi-level complex structure unfolding down the slope on the opposite site of the house. Making the best of the slanted site, the architects opened the interiors to the natural light and extensive landscapes. Vertical panes along and across the slope form the main structure, holding various elements of the house on different levels. Light and richly glazed, they appear as a combination of rooms with a view, all of which are fluidly interconnected, from the basement with a sauna and fitness room as well as a roofed outdoor area, to the attic floor housing the parents' space. The way all volumes are shifted horizontally along the hill creates many balconies, varying in size, some of which are roofed. The floor-to-ceiling windows open all rooms onto the picturesque view. The materials used for the interior design were selected to enhance the spatial continuity within the house.

Die Fassade an der Straßenseite, wo sich der Haupteingang befindet, kann trügerisch sein. Es besteht aus drei rechteckigen Blöcken, die auf zwei Ebenen ausgerichtet sind und außer der Glastür keine Öffnungen aufweisen. Es ist nicht zu sehen, dass sich die komplexe mehrstöckige Struktur entlang eines Hügels auf der gegenüberliegenden Seite erstreckt. Die Architekten haben das Beste aus der Hanglage herausgeholt und die Innenräume für das natürliche Licht und die weite Landschaft geöffnet. Die Struktur wird von großen vertikalen Fensterscheiben dominiert, die den verschiedenen Teilen der Villa Einheit verleihen. Diese großen Fenster, die eine helle Einheit bilden, verbinden die verschiedenen Räume: das Untergeschoss, das mit einer Sauna, einem Fitnessraum und einer überdachten Terrasse ausgestattet ist, über die oberen Stockwerken bis zum Dachgeschoss, in dem sich das Elternschlafzimmer befindet. Die horizontale Anordnung der Böden entlang des Hangs hat es ermöglicht, unterschiedlich große, teilweise überdachte Balkone zu erschaffen. Alle Räume öffnen sich dank ihrer großen Glaswände zur besonders malerischen Landschaft. Die für die Innenarchitektur verwendeten Materialien wurden so gewählt, dass die räumliche Kontinuität innerhalb des Hauses verstärkt wird.

La façade du côté rue, où se trouve l'entrée principale, peut être trompeuse. Elle se compose de trois blocs rectangulaires alignés sur deux niveaux et dépourvus de toute ouverture à l'exception de la porte vitrée. On ne soupçonne rien de la structure complexe à plusieurs étages qui se déploie, du côté opposé, le long d'une colline. Les architectes ont su tirer le meilleur de l'inclinaison et ont ouvert les intérieurs à la lumière naturelle et aux vastes paysages. La structure côté pente est rythmée par de grandes baies vitrées qui donnent une unité aux différentes parties de la villa. Ces grandes fenêtres qui forment un ensemble léger relient entre elles les différentes pièces de la villa depuis le sous-sol, équipé d'un sauna, d'une salle de fitness et d'une terrasse couverte jusqu'aux étages supérieurs et même au grenier qui abrite la chambre des parents. La disposition horizontale des étages le long de la colline a permis l'installation de balcons de taille variable dont certains sont couverts. Toutes les pièces s'ouvrent sur le paysage particulièrement pittoresque grâce à leurs grandes parois vitrées. Les matériaux utilisés pour l'aménagement intérieur ont été choisis de manière à renforcer la continuité spatiale au sein de la maison.

Interiors Innenräume Intérieurs

Terrace view

Blick auf die Terrasse

Vue sur la terrasse

HOUSE E

ARTEMIS, GREECE

Home to a small young family, House E stands close to the Aegean Sea coast. The ultimate goal was to achieve comfortable and high-quality living spaces, both indoor and outdoor, but also to strike a balance between intimacy and openings to the views. The building is a composite construction with a minimum footprint on the small plot it occupies. Based on a reinforced concrete structure, the house is two floors high and is split into visually contrasting parts. The smaller and mostly glazed bottom cube holds a traditionally shaped top floor covered with a pitched roof. The upper cantilevered volume tricks the eye, as it seems to be floating above the ground. It is divided into two high-ceiling bedrooms with private loggias, which have full-height openable shutter panels to enjoy the seascape, as well as a bathroom planned around a stairwell and a study. The transparent space on the ground floor offers living and dining areas which are seamlessly connected to a terrace with a small pool and a garden. The architects successfully employed a playful juxtaposition of solid and light, closed and open.

Haus E, das eine kleine Familie beherbergt, liegt in der Nähe der Ägäisküste. Das Ziel der Architekten war es, einen komfortablen und qualitativ hochwertigen Wohnraum sowohl innen als auch außen zu bieten, aber auch ein Gleichgewicht zwischen Privatsphäre und Offenheit für die außergewöhnliche Aussicht zu finden. Die Villa ist ein zusammengesetztes Gebäude mit einem minimalen Grundflächenbedarf auf dem kleinen Grundstück, das es belegt. Das um eine Stahlbetonstruktur herum gebaute Haus hat zwei Stockwerke und ist in mehrere, visuell kontrastierende Teile unterteilt. Der untere Kubus, der kleiner und verglast ist, trägt ein etwas traditioneller gestaltetes Obergeschoss mit einem Schrägdach. Der auskragende obere Teil sorgt für einen Trompe-l'oeil-Effekt, da er über dem Boden zu schweben scheint. Er ist in zwei hohe Räume mit privaten Loggien unterteilt, um die Meereslandschaft zu genießen und beherbergt auch ein um ein Treppenhaus herum entworfenes Badezimmer und ein Büro. Der transparente Raum im Erdgeschoss beherbergt ein Wohn- und ein Esszimmer, die nahtlos an eine Terrasse mit einem kleinen Swimmingpool und Garten angeschlossen sind. Den Architekten ist es gelungen, massive und leichte, geschlossene und offene Elemente spielerisch nebeneinander zu stellen.

La maison E, qui abrite une petite famille, se trouve près de la côte de la mer Égée. L'ambition des architectes était d'offrir un espace confortable et de grande qualité tant à l'intérieur qu'à l'extérieur, mais également de trouver un équilibre entre intimité et ouverture sur la vue exceptionnelle. Le bâtiment est un édifice composite avec une empreinte minimale sur la petite parcelle qu'il occupe. Construite autour d'une structure en béton armé, la maison comprend deux étages. Elle est divisée en plusieurs parties visuellement contrastées. Le cube inférieur, plus petit et équipé des baies vitrées, soutient un étage supérieur de forme traditionnelle recouvert d'un toit incliné. La partie supérieure en porte-à-faux créé un effet trompe-l'œil car elle semble flotter au-dessus du sol. Elle est partagée en deux chambres à haut plafond avec des loggias privées ornées de volets ouvrables sur toute la hauteur pour profiter du paysage marin. Elle abrite aussi une salle de bains conçue autour d'une cage d'escalier et un bureau. L'espace transparent du rez-de-chaussée accueille une salle de séjour et une salle à manger qui sont reliées de manière transparente à une terrasse avec une petite piscine et un jardin. Les architectes ont réussi à juxtaposer de manière ludique des éléments massifs et légers, fermés et ouverts.

ARCHITECTS: BUERGER KATSOTA ARCHITECTS /// **COMPLETION:** 2019 /// **FLOOR AREA:** 65 M² (700 FT²) /// **PHOTOS :** YIORGIS YEROLYMBOS, BUERGER KATSOTA ARCHITECTS

Terrace view

Blick auf die Terrasse

Vue sur la terrasse

Entrance Eingangsbereich Entrée

Exterior view Außenansicht Vue extérieure

Staircase Treppe Escalier

Interiors Innenräume Intérieurs

Interiors Innenräume Intérieurs

TM HOUSE

COLIMA, MEXICO

Creating a building that would constantly evoke the idea of an unending vacation was at the core of designing this single-storey residence for a family of four. Inspired by the tropical paradise of the Mexican pacific, the project was defined by the climate, topography, and context. Referring to one of the particularities of the Mexican architectural tradition, namely the deliberate ambiguity between interior and exterior, TM House's structure blurs this division. Its complex and dispersed horizontal structure has two focal points. One of them is a circular patio, which redirects the airflow from spaces integrated with the terrace towards the sleeping areas. It also encircles an island of palm trees providing shade. The second is the living area, based on a platform to protect the house from recurring floods, opening boldly to extensive outdoor terraces and a sloped garden. The finishes in the walls, roofs, and lattices were handcrafted by local workmen to add sophistication to the contemporary creation. They marry traditions with today's design language. The architects also implemented a sustainable solution in the construction of the roof to reduce the absorption of solar radiation and contribute to thermal insulation.

Dieses einstöckige Wohnhaus für eine vierköpfige Familie war von Anfang an mit dem Ziel entworfen worden, das Gefühl von einem niemals endenden Urlaub zu vermitteln. Inspiriert vom tropischen Paradies der mexikanischen Pazifikküste, bestimmten das Klima, die Topografie und der Kontext das Konzept. Als Hommage an die mexikanische Architekturtradition der bewussten Ambivalenz zwischen innen und außen hebt die Struktur des TM-Hauses diese Trennung auf. Diese sich über eine weite Fläche erstreckende, komplexe und horizontale Struktur hat zwei zentrale Punkte. Einen davon bildet der kreisförmige, der den Luftstrom von den in die Terrasse integrierten Räumen in die Schlafzimmer umleitet. Dieser Innenhof hat in seiner Mitte eine Insel mit Palmen, die naturlichen Schatten bieten. Der zweite Schwerpunkt ist das Wohnzimmer, das auf einer erhöhten Plattform gebaut wurde, um das Haus vor Überschwemmungen zu schützen, und das sich kühn zu großen Außenterrassen und einem schräg abfallenden Garten hin öffnet. Die Wände, Dächer und Spaliere wurden von lokalen Handwerkern handgefertigt, um der Architektur einen Hauch von Raffinesse zu verleihen und die Tradition mit der heutigen Designsprache zu verbinden. Die Architekten realisierten eine nachhaltige Lösung bei der Konstruktion des Daches, um die Absorption der Sonnenstrahlung zu reduzieren und die Wärmedämmung zu erhöhen.

Cette résidence de plain-pied pour une famille de quatre personnes a été conçue dès le départ comme un lieu de villégiature où l'on aurait le sentiment de vivre des vacances sans fin. Au cœur du paradis tropical de la côte Pacifique mexicaine, le bâtiment a été inspiré par le climat, la topographie et le contexte. En hommage à une tradition bien établie de l'architecture mexicaine, à savoir l'ambiguïté assumée entre intérieur et extérieur, la structure de TM House fait sans cesse passer les habitants de l'un à l'autre. Sa structure horizontale assez complexe et dispersée comporte deux points centraux. L'un d'eux est un patio circulaire qui redirige le flux d'air des espaces intégrés à la terrasse vers les chambres à coucher. Ce patio a en son centre un îlot de palmiers qui fournissent de l'ombre naturelle.
Le second point central est la salle de séjour, bâtie sur une plateforme surélevée pour protéger la maison des inondations récurrentes et qui s'ouvre audacieusement sur de vastes terrasses extérieures et sur un jardin en pente. Les finitions des murs, des toits et des treillis ont été réalisées à la main par des ouvriers locaux pour ajouter une touche de sophistication à la création contemporaine et marier les traditions avec le langage du design d'aujourd'hui. Les architectes ont utilisé une solution compatible avec le développement durable pour la construction du toit afin de réduire l'absorption du rayonnement solaire et de renforcer l'isolation thermique.

ARCHITECTS: CDM I CASAS DE MÉXICO /// **COMPLETION:** 2017 /// **FURTHER PARTICIPANTS:** JAVIER DUEÑAS, DELFINO LOZANO, DANIEL VILLALBA, RODRIGO CARREON (ARCHITECTS) /// **FLOOR AREA:** 769 M^2 (8,280 FT^2) /// **PHOTOS:** RORY GARDINER

Entrance Eingangsbereich Entrée

Patio

Terrace view

Blick auf die Terrasse

Vue sur la terrasse

Interiors Innenräume Intérieurs

Façade opening up towards the garden

Fassade an der Gartenseite

Façade côté jardin

VILLA B

ALDRANS, AUSTRIA

Villa B, also called "Pleated B Villa" by the architects, is a visually striking combination of simple forms and massive materials. Presenting itself entirely differently from each side, the house is reminiscent of an origami object. The dramatic bends of the walls and the shifted roof at full height inside the house define the interiors. Following the roof slopes, the floor plan is divided into different height zones, creating dynamic spaces in each part of the villa. As all walls are punctured by openings in different sizes and on various levels, the natural light adds additional effects, playing on the surfaces and internal folds. The central staircase is the element that organises the house and divides its large open spaces. From outside, sitting among hilly fields, the structure appears as a solid form, which in spite of its scale and geometric forms immerses itself into the natural landscape. On the one hand the shape refers to the terrain's topography; on the other, it relates to the local architecture, particularly through the street façade. The frame running along the house's profile creates intimacy and connects it with its surroundings.

Die Villa B, die von ihren Architekten auch „plissierte Villa B" genannt wird, verbindet harmonisch eine große Einfachheit der Formen mit einer gewissen Monumentalität der Materialien. Die Villa bietet auf jeder Seite ein völlig unterschiedliches Aussehen und erinnert an eine Origami-Faltung. Die ineinandergreifenden Wände und das zum Inneren des Hauses hin geneigte Dach prägen die Räume. Je nach der Neigung des Daches ist die Villa in mehrere Teile unterschiedlicher Höhe unterteilt, wodurch in jedem von ihnen dynamische Räume entstehen. Da alle Wände von unterschiedlich großen Fenstern durchbrochen sind, die sich auf verschiedenen Ebenen befinden, stellt das natürliche Licht durch das Spiel auf den Oberflächen und in den Ecken einen zusätzlichen Reiz dar. Die zentrale Treppe ist das Element, das das Haus strukturiert und die großen offenen Räume unterteilt. Von außen, inmitten von hügeligen Feldern, vermittelt das Haus den Eindruck eines massiven Blocks, der trotz seiner Größe und geometrischen Formen fröhlich in die natürliche Landschaft eintaucht. Die Formen der Villa entsprechen der Topographie des Geländes; außerdem nimmt sie bestimmte Elemente der lokalen Architektur auf, insbesondere für die Straßenfassade. Der weiße Rahmen, der das ganze Haus umfasst, schafft Privatheit und verbindet es auch mit der Natur.

La Villa B, également appelée «Villa plissée B» par ses architectes, combine harmonieusement une grande simplicité de formes avec une certaine monumentalité des matériaux. La villa offre un aspect totalement différent de chacun des côtés et fait penser à un pliage en origami. L'enchevêtrement des murs et le toit incliné vers l'intérieur de la maison marquent les espaces intérieurs. Suivant l'inclinaison du toit, la villa est divisée en plusieurs parties de hauteur variable, ce qui créé des espaces dynamiques dans chacune d'entre elles. Comme tous les murs sont percés de fenêtres de taille distincte installées à différents niveaux, la lumière naturelle ajoute une touche supplémentaire en jouant sur les surfaces et les plis internes. L'escalier central est l'élément qui structure la maison et divise ses grands espaces ouverts. De l'extérieur, plantée au milieu de champs vallonnés, la maison donne l'impression d'un bloc massif qui, malgré ses dimensions et ses formes géométriques, s'immerge avec bonheur dans le paysage naturel. Les formes de la villa s'inscrivent dans la topographie du terrain ; par ailleurs, elle emprunte certains éléments à l'architecture locale, notamment pour sa façade côté rue. Le cadre qui entoure la maison crée une certaine intimité et fait le lien avec la nature environnante.

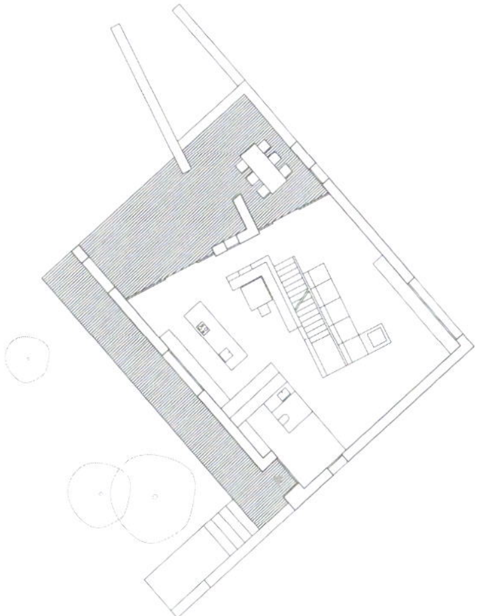

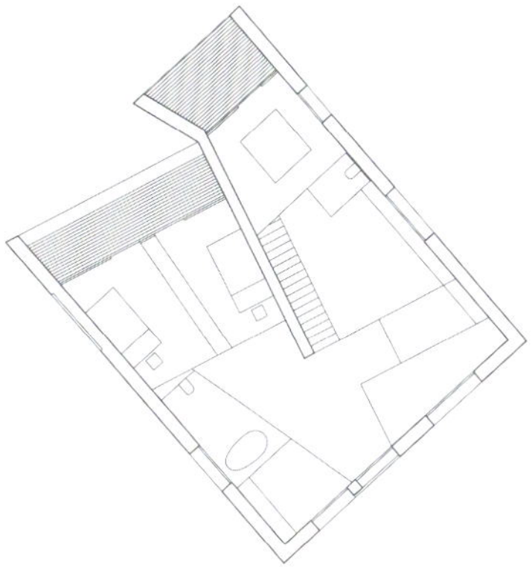

Garage

Ground and first floor plans

Grundrisse Erdgeschoss und Obergeschoss

Plans du rez-de-chaussée et du premier étage

Interiors Innenräume Intérieurs

Exterior view Außenansicht Vue extérieure

Façade opening up towards the garden

Fassade an der Gartenseite

Façade côté jardin

Sketches Skizzen Esquisses

ARCHITECTS: AHAD ARCHITEKTEN /// **COMPLETION:** 2018 /// **FLOOR AREA:** 560 M² (6,028 FT²) /// **PHOTOS:** ADRIAN SCHULZ

HOUSE NALDO

WOLFSBURG, GERMANY

The House Naldo, designed for the Brazilian football star, is located in the immediate vicinity of the Holy Spirit Church designed by Alvar Aalto. Both this iconic building dating from 1962 and Le Corbusier's crafts culture influenced the interior and exterior design of the L-shaped house. The façade is linear towards the street and opens up towards the garden like a tribune. White plaster surfaces contrast with parts of the façade that were modelled with bronze-coloured brush strokes. Room-high windows with bronze-coloured, anodised frames harmonise with the oak entrance door. On the ground floor you will find a spacious guest area and the main living rooms. They evolve fluidly around a high central air volume and a gallery with a transparent railing as well as windows and skylights that direct natural light into the interior of the house. All rooms on the upper floor have direct access to the loggia, which extends along the entire length of the house. On the ground floor, a glass façade on the garden side connects the living rooms with the outdoor area equipped with a swimming pool, which is partially covered by the protruding corner area of the first floor. All bedrooms have their own bathrooms, and the children's bedrooms are tiled with tiles in soft pink and pale green hues according to Le Corbusier's theory of colours.

Das für den brasilianischen Fußballstar entworfene Haus Naldo liegt in direkter Nachbarschaft zur von Alvar Aalto entworfenen Heilig-Geist Kirche. Sowohl dieser ikonische Bau von 1962 als auch Le Corbusiers Handwerkskultur beeinflussten die Innen- und Außengestaltung des L-förmigen Hauses. Zur Straße ist die Fassade gradlinig, zum Garten hin öffnet sie sich wie eine Tribüne. Weiße Putzflächen kontrastieren mit Fassadenteilflächen, die mit bronzefarbenem Besenstrich modelliert wurden. Raumhohe Fenster mit bronzefarbenen, eloxierten Rahmen harmonieren mit der Eingangstür aus Eichenholz. Im Erdgeschoss befinden sich ein großzügiger Gästebereich sowie die Hauptwohnräume. Sie entwickeln sich fließend um einen hohen zentralen Luftraum und eine Galerie mit transparentem Geländer sowie Fenstern und Oberlichtern, die über beide Geschosse natürliches Licht ins Innerste des Hauses leiten. Alle Räume des Obergeschosses haben Zugang zur Loggia, die sich über die gesamte Länge des Hauses erstreckt. Eine Glasfassade an der Gartenseite des Erdgeschosses verbindet den Wohnbereich mit dem Außenbereich mit Swimmingpool, der teilweise vom ausladenden Eckbereich des ersten Geschosses überdacht ist. Alle Schlafzimmer verfügen über ein eigenes Badezimmer, die der Kinder sind mit nach Le Corbusiers Farbenlehre gestalteten Kacheln in zartem Rosa und Blassgrün gefliest.

La Maison Naldo, conçue pour la star brésilienne du football, est située à proximité immédiate de l'église du Saint-Esprit conçue par Alvar Aalto. Ce bâtiment emblématique datant de 1962 et les enseignements de Le Corbusier ont tous deux influencé la conception intérieure et extérieure de cette maison en forme de L. Côté rue, la façade est linéaire tandis qu'elle s'ouvre comme une tribune côté jardin. Des surfaces en plâtre blanc forment un contraste avec d'autres parties des façades qui ont été décorées couleur bronze à des coups de pinceaux. Des fenêtres du plancher au plafond aux cadres anodisés couleur bronze forment un ensemble harmonieux avec la porte d'entrée en chêne. Le rez-de-chaussée est occupé par un espace réservé aux invités et les salles de séjour. Ces pièces sont construites autour d'un espace central vide et d'une galerie équipée d'une balustrade transparente ainsi que de fenêtres et de lucarnes qui aspirent la lumière naturelle vers l'intérieur de la maison. Toutes les chambres de l'étage supérieur disposent d'un accès à la loggia qui s'étend sur toute la longueur de la maison. Une façade en verre au rez-de-chaussée, côté, relie les pièces de séjour à l'espace extérieur doté d'une piscine qui est en partie couverte par la zone d'angle en saillie du premier étage. Toutes les chambres ont une salle de bain particulière. Les chambres des enfants sont carrelées de carreaux rose tendre et vert pâle selon la théorie des couleurs de Le Corbusier.

Street façade

Fassade an der Straßenseite

Façade côté rue

Terrace view

Blick auf die Terrasse

Vue sur la terrasse

Pool Swimmingpool Piscine

Interiors Innenräume Intérieurs

Façade opening up towards the garden

Fassade an der Gartenseite

Façade côté jardin

CHS HOUSE

SANTIAGO, CHILE

The main goal of the project was to find a perfect solution for a double use of the house – both as a residence and a workspace. The fact that the site is located in a low-density area did not make it easier but inspired the architects to use the ground level for a clear division of spaces and to align it with the neighbouring architecture. As a result, the house is arranged on three levels – a ground floor transition block mediates between the basement office and the top floor with bedrooms. This middle part, with access to the garden, was planned by minimalising structural elements and maximising transparent elements. Additionally, one of the corners is transformed into a three-level void, which also serves as a patio that provides natural light to the workspace. The low yet colossal volume was built of materials adjusted to the region's strong seismic activity. Both outside and inside, some of the elements in the mainly concrete structures are coated in wood, like the mobile wooden screens on top floor windows or the interior floors made of national Raulí wood.

Das Hauptziel des Projekts war es, die perfekte Lösung für eine gemischte Nutzung des Hauses, sowohl als Familienhaus als auch als Arbeitsplatz zu finden. Die Tatsache, dass das Gelände in einem Gebiet mit geringer Dichte liegt, machte die Sache nicht einfacher, aber sie veranlasste die Architekten, das Erdgeschoss zu nutzen, um die Räume deutlich zu teilen und den Stil der Villa an die Architektur des Gebietes anzupassen. Daher ist das Haus drei Stockwerke hoch - eine Übergangsebene im Erdgeschoss dient als Zwischengeschoss zwischen dem Büro im Untergeschoss und dem für die Schlafzimmer bestimmten Obergeschoss. Dieser Zwischenteil, der den Zugang zum Garten ermöglicht, wurde so entworfen, dass die solide Struktur minimiert und die transparenten Elemente maximiert wurden. Eine der Ecken der Villa bildet einen leeren Raum, der sich über die drei Stockwerke erstreckt und als Terrasse dient, um natürliches Licht in das Büro im Untergeschoss zu bringen. Das eher niedrige, aber imposante Gebäude wurde mit Materialien gebaut, die an die hohe seismische Aktivität in diesem Gebiet angepasst sind. Sowohl außen als auch innen sind einige Elemente der Betonstruktur mit Holz verkleidet, wie zum Beispiel die beweglichen Fensterläden im obersten Stockwerk oder die Innenböden aus dem nationalen Raulí-Holz.

L'objectif principal du projet était de trouver la solution parfaite pour un usage mixte de la maison, à la fois comme résidence familiale et comme espace de travail. Le fait que le site soit situé dans une zone à faible densité n'a pas facilité les choses mais cela a incité les architectes à utiliser le rez-de-chaussée pour partager distinctement les pièces et à aligner le style de la villa sur l'architecture du voisinage. En conséquence, la maison s'élève sur trois étages - un niveau de transition au rez-de-chaussée sert d'intermédiaire entre le bureau du sous-sol et l'étage supérieur réservé aux chambres. Cette partie intermédiaire qui donne accès au jardin a été conçue en minimisant la structure solide et en maximisant les éléments transparents. L'un des coins de la villa forme un espace vide qui s'étend sur les trois étages et sert ainsi de patio pour apporter de la lumière naturelle au bureau du sous-sol. Le bâtiment, assez bas mais imposant, a été construit avec des matériaux adaptés à la forte activité sismique de la région. Tant à l'extérieur qu'à l'intérieur, certains éléments de la structure en béton sont recouverts de bois, comme les volets mobiles des fenêtres du dernier étage ou les planchers intérieurs en raulí, le bois national.

ARCHITECTS: CHAURIYE STAGER ARQUITECTOS /// **COMPLETION:** 2018 /// **FURTHER :** BEATRIZ STÄGER, RODRIGO CHAURIYE, VINCENZO CASTELLO, FELIPE ASTUDILLO /// **FLOOR AREA:** 480 M² (5,170 FT²) /// **PHOTOS:** PABLO CASALS

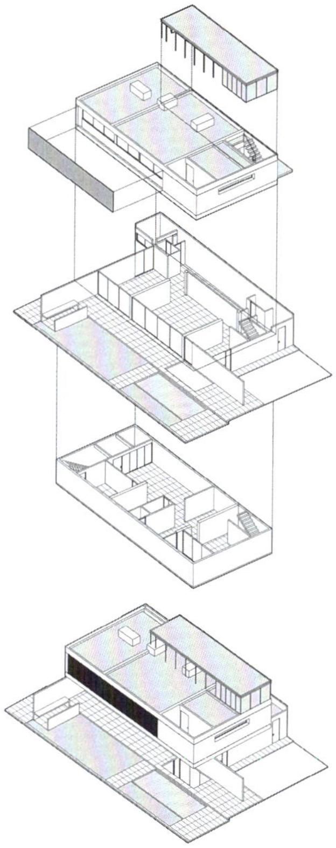

Street façade

Fassade an der Straßenseite

Façade côté rue

Section Schnitt Section

Kitchen Küche Cuisine

Terrace view

Blick auf die Terrasse

Vue sur la terrasse

ARCHITECTS: CHRIST.CHRIST. ASSOCIATED ARCHITECTS GMBH /// **COMPLETION:** 2018 /// **FLOOR AREA:** 444 M² (4,780 FT²) /// **PHOTOS:** THOMAS HERRMANN

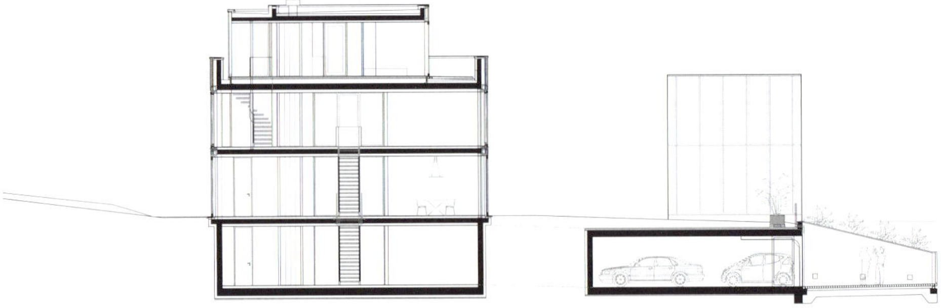

HOUSE E

WIESBADEN, GERMANY

House E is a fascinating ensemble of two cubic structures connected by an underground tunnel. The residential building has a façade of muted grey bricks, the pavilion, which is used as a private office, is fully mirrored. These two cubic buildings are identical in form, but differ significantly in the choice of materials and colours. They are placed in the middle of a garden plateau that has been set up three metres above street level. The spatial arrangement of the residential building is organised around the entrance hall and the central staircase. The reduced number of partition walls between the floors and the natural daylight entering through large windows enhance the impression of a very spacious house. The top floor, which is accessed via a separate half-spiral staircase, is an intimate sleeping area with an open bathroom and a dressing room. Just as the glass façades allow a view through the glass pavilion, the brick house is reflected in its twin in an interesting way. The walls of the latter constantly play between transparency and reflection, absorbing the path of the sunlight: the appearance of the pavilion therefore varies according to the time of day and the angle of reflection.

Haus E ist ein reizvolles Ensemble aus zwei kubischen Baukörpern, die durch einen unterirdischen Tunnel verbunden sind. Die Fassade des Wohnhauses besteht aus Backsteinen in gedecktem Grau. Der Pavillon, der als Privatbüro genutzt wird, ist vollflächig verspiegelt. Diese beiden kubischen Gebäude sind in ihrer Form identisch, unterscheiden sich aber grundlegend in der Wahl der Materialien und Farben. Sie sind platziert inmitten eines Gartenplateaus, das drei Meter über der Straßenebene errichtet wurde. Im Wohnhaus ordnen sich die Räume rund um die Eingangshalle und die zentral platzierte Treppe. Durch die reduzierte Anzahl von Trennwänden zwischen den Stockwerken sowie dem natürlichen Tageslichteinfall durch große Fensterflächen verstärkt sich die Anmutung eines sehr geräumigen Wohnhauses. Im Staffelgeschoss, dem obersten Stockwerk, das über eine separate halbkreisförmige Treppe erreicht wird, befindet sich der Schlafbereich mit offenem Badezimmer und Ankleide. So, wie die Glasfassaden den Blick durch den Glaspavillon ermöglichen, spiegelt sich das Backsteinhaus auf interessante Weise in seinem Zwilling wider. Die Wände des letzteren spielen ständig zwischen Transparenz und Reflexion und absorbieren den Weg des Sonnenlichts: Das Aussehen des Pavillons variiert also je nach Tageszeit und Reflexionswinkel.

La maison E est un charmant ensemble de deux structures cubiques reliées par un tunnel souterrain. Le bâtiment dont la façade est en briques gris clair est à usage résidentiel ; l'autre, avec des miroirs sur toute sa surface, est un pavillon utilisé comme bureau privé. De forme identique, mais très différents dans le choix des matériaux et des couleurs, ces deux édifices cubiques se dressent au milieu d'un jardin surélevé de 3 mètres par rapport à la rue. Ils occupent les bords opposés d'une parcelle recouverte d'herbe. La disposition spatiale de la partie résidentielle s'organise autour du hall d'entrée et d'un escalier central. Le nombre limité de cloisons entre les étages ainsi que la lumière naturelle abondante qui passe par d'amples baies vitrées en font une maison très spacieuse. Le dernier étage, auquel on accède par un escalier en demi-cercle séparé, est une chambre à coucher intimiste avec une salle de bain et un dressing intégrés. Tout comme les façades vitrées permettent de voir à travers le pavillon en verre, la maison en briques se reflète de façon intéressante sur sa jumelle. Les murs de ce dernier jouent sans cesse entre transparence et réflexion et ils absorbent la trajectoire de la lumière solaire : L'aspect du pavillon varie ainsi selon l'heure du jour et l'angle de réflexion.

General view

Gesamtansicht

Vue générale

Section Schnitt Section

Interiors Innenräume Intérieurs

Staircase Treppe Escalier

General view Gesamtansicht Vue générale

Passage Durchgang Passage

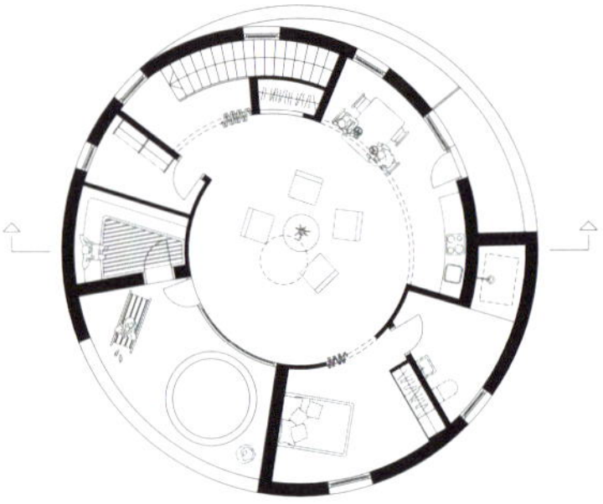

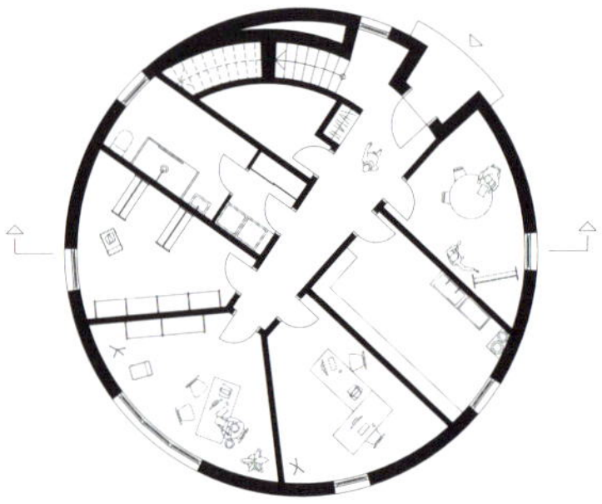

ARCHITECTS: CHRISTOPH HESSE ARCHITEKTEN /// **COMPLETION:** 2016 /// **FLOOR AREA:** 180 M^2 (1,940 FT^2) ///
PHOTOS: DEIMEL + WITTMAR, CHRISTOPH HESSE

VILLA F

MEDEBACH, GERMANY

Challenged by a client's unusual wish for a spherical and thus energy-efficient house, the architect designed an emblematic, striking cylindrical shape. The house has two floors – with office spaces on the ground level and the residence part on the upper, loft-like floor. While the shape of the roof echoes the topography of the nearby slopes and mountains, numerous windows, a loggia with a whirlpool, and a balcony allow a 360-degree panorama of the surrounding landscape. Connecting the house with the nature was crucial for the owner, a talented inventor who has an agricultural background. Energy efficiency and environmental issues were equally important for the owner, as he and his father are both pioneers of biogas technology, which is also employed here to make the house self-sufficient. The heating supply and disposal of the waste both rely on the biogas plant. The success of this solution has led to the creation of an entire network based on the same model that connects all households in the village. Another of the owner's contributions was the decoration of the bright curved façade with cladding made of stones from a nearby stream.

Dem ungewöhnlichen Wunsch eines Bauherrn nach einem rundförmigen und damit energieeffizienten Haus zufolge, entwarf der Architekt eine emblematisch wirkungsvolle zylindrische Gestalt. Das Haus hat zwei Etagen, mit Büros im Erdgeschoss und dem Wohnteil im Obergeschoss, das als Dachgeschoss ausgelegt ist. Die Form des einseitig geneigten Daches fügt sich in die Topographie der umliegenden Hänge und Berge ein. Zahlreiche Fenster sowie eine mit einem Whirlpool ausgestattete Loggia und ein Balkon bieten einen 360-Grad-Blick auf die umliegende Landschaft. Die Verbindung zwischen dem Haus und der Natur war für den Besitzer, einen talentierten Erfinder mit landwirtschaftlichem Hintergrund, von entscheidender Bedeutung. Energieeffizienz und Umweltfragen waren für ihn ebenso wichtig, da er und sein Vater beide Pioniere der Biogastechnologie sind, die hier zur Selbstversorgung des Hauses eingesetzt wird. Sowohl die Wärmeversorgung als auch die Abfallentsorgung hängen von der Biogasanlage ab. Der Erfolg dieser Lösung hat zur Schaffung eines ganzen Netzwerks geführt, das auf dem gleichen Modell basiert und alle Haushalte im Dorf miteinander verbindet. Der Eigentümer hat auch der Dekoration der hellen, runden Fassade seinen Stempel aufgedrückt, indem er eine Verkleidung aus Steinen eines nahe gelegenen Baches wählte.

Pour répondre au souhait insolite d'un client d'avoir une maison ronde et donc à faible consommation d'énergie, l'architecte a conçu une forme cylindrique à la fois emblématique et performante. La maison comporte deux étages, avec des bureaux au rez-de-chaussée et la partie résidentielle à l'étage supérieur qui est aménagé en loft. La forme du toit incliné d'un seul côté se fond dans la topographie des pentes et des montagnes environnantes. De nombreuses fenêtres, une loggia équipé d'un jacuzzi et un balcon offrent un panorama à 360 degrés sur le paysage alentour. Le lien entre la maison et la nature était crucial pour le propriétaire, un inventeur de talent qui a une formation agricole. L'efficacité énergétique et les questions environnementales étaient tout aussi importantes pour lui, car son père et lui sont tous deux des pionniers de la technologie du biogaz qui est utilisée ici pour rendre la maison autosuffisante. L'approvisionnement en chauffage et l'élimination des déchets dépendent tous deux de l'installation de biogaz. Le succès de cette solution a conduit à la création d'un réseau entier basé sur le même modèle qui relie tous les ménages du village. Le propriétaire a également imprimé sa marque sur la décoration de la façade arrondie et lumineuse en choisissant un revêtement en pierres provenant d'un ruisseau voisin.

General view Gesamtansicht Vue générale

Ground floor and first floor plans

Grundrisse Erdgeschoss und Obergeschoss

Plans du rez-de-chaussée et du premier étage

Interiors Innenräume Intérieurs

Loggia with a whirlpool

Loggia mit Jacuzzi

Loggia avec jacuzzi

Exterior view

Außenansicht

Vue extérieure

WOHNHAUS KÖLN HAHNWALD

COLOGNE, GERMANY

Strange as it may sound, this modern villa was primarily designed to house a swimming pool complemented by a wellness area, which are quite uncommonly located on the upper floor. The ground floor, envisioned as a comfortable open sequence of rooms, is integrated through floor-to-ceiling windows with the garden and a terrace. The owner initially wished to incorporate the pool into an existing house on the site but as that proved to be impossible, the building was demolished. The architect envisioned instead a rhombic shape and placed it in line with the street and neighbouring houses. This solution enabled a spacious residence that takes the form of two massive volumes in an expressive shift, creating an extensive terrace on one side, and on the other a small roof over the entrance to an underground garage (connected with a cellar divided into several small spaces). The dynamic shape is enhanced by the natural stone cladding of grey quartzite. Rhythmically arranged longitudinal stripes in various hues emphasise the sharp angles and horizontal orientation of the structure. To create visual continuity, the same stone was used in the interiors for all floors, bathrooms, and the swimming pool area.

So merkwürdig es auch klingen mag, wurde diese moderne Villa vor allem für und um ein Schwimmbecken und einen Wellnessbereich herum entworfen, die sich beide ungewöhnlicherweise im Obergeschoss befinden. Das Erdgeschoss, das als eine Reihe offener und komfortabler Räume gestaltet wurde, ist durch raumhohe Fenster in den Garten und die Terrasse integriert. Ursprünglich wollte die Eigentümerin den Pool in einem bereits auf dem Gelände befindlichen Haus bauen lassen, aber da sich dies als unmöglich erwies, wurde das Gebäude abgerissen. Stattdessen entwarf der Architekt eine rautenförmige Villa und setzte sie in Einklang mit der Straße und den Nachbarhäusern. Diese Lösung führte zu einem geräumigen Wohnhaus, das aus zwei imposanten, leicht versetzten Stockwerken besteht, wobei auf der einen Seite eine große Terrasse und auf der anderen Seite ein Vordach über der Einfahrt zu einer Tiefgarage (die sich zu einem in mehrere kleine Räume unterteilten Keller öffnet) geschaffen wurde. Das dynamische Erscheinungsbild des Gebäudes wird durch die Natursteinverkleidung aus grauem Quarzit verstärkt. Rhythmisch angeordnete Längsstreifen in verschiedenen Farben unterstreichen die scharfen Winkel und die horizontale Ausrichtung der Struktur. Um eine visuelle Kontinuität zu schaffen, wurde im Inneren für alle Böden, Badezimmer und den Swimmingpool derselbe Stein verwendet.

Aussi curieux que cela puisse paraître, Cette villa moderne a été conçue avant tout pour abriter une piscine agrémentée d'un espace de bien-être situés tous deux, de façon insolite, à l'étage supérieur. Le rez-de-chaussée, conçu comme une suite de pièces ouvertes et confortables, est intégré au jardin et à la terrasse par des fenêtres allant du sol au plafond. La propriétaire souhaitait initialement faire aménager la piscine dans une maison déjà présente sur le site, mais comme cela s'est avéré impossible, le bâtiment a été démoli. L'architecte a imaginé à la place un édifice en forme de losange et l'a placé dans l'alignement de la rue et des maisons voisines. De cette solution est née une résidence spacieuse formée deux étages imposants légèrement décalés, ce qui crée une vaste terrasse d'un côté, un auvent au-dessus de l'entrée d'un garage souterrain (qui donne sur une cave divisée en plusieurs petits espaces) de l'autre côté. L'aspect dynamique du bâtiment est renforcé par le revêtement en pierre naturelle de quartzite gris. Des bandes longitudinales disposées de manière rythmée et de différentes teintes soulignent les angles vifs et l'orientation horizontale de la structure. Pour créer une continuité visuelle, la même pierre a été utilisée à l'intérieur pour tous les sols, les salles de bains et la piscine.

ARCHITECTS: CORNEILLE UEDINGSLOHMANN ARCHITEKTEN /// **COMPLETION:** 2016 /// **FLOOR AREA:** 266 M² (2,860 FT²) ///
PHOTOS: MICHAEL NEUHAUS

Street façade

Fassade an der Straßenseite

Façade côté rue

Entrance Eingangsbereich Entrée

Pool Swimmingpool Piscine

Terrace view

Blick auf die Terrasse

Vue sur la terrasse

VILLA GEEF

SONDRIO, ITALY

Built on an extensive plot surrounded by stunning mountains and vineyards, Villa Geef celebrates the beauty of landscapes. The single-floor house, clearly divided into two parts, has immersed itself into the natural context. One side of the building is occupied by the garage and rooms for guests, the other by the owner's residence. Both are connected with a roofed porch, which is in line with the entrance to the plot. The structure's relation to its surroundings is also developed through its light and transparent construction, which dominates neither the nature nor the local architecture. The minimalistic design is enhanced by the use of glass, wood, and stone. Natural materials play a particularly important role on the exterior walls and floors, where the architects utilised local "Serpentino" stone. Inside, wooden floors work well with the warm tones of the walls and furniture. The architects' goal was to create a cosy home to enjoy the natural scenery, yet significantly glazed walls also fill the house with natural light. The outdoor space, partly roofed and offering a pool, creates a fluid transition between the interiors and the garden.

Die Villa Geef wurde auf einem weiten, von Bergen und überwältigenden Weinbergen umgebenen Grundstück gebaut. Ihr Standort wurde aufgrund der einzigartigen Aussicht gewählt, die er über die Landschaft bietet. Das einstöckige Haus, das klar in zwei Teile gegliedert ist, ist in seine natürliche Umgebung eingebettet. Auf der einen Seite des Gebäudes befinden sich die Garage und die Gästezimmer, auf der anderen der Wohnsitz des Eigentümers. Beide sind durch eine überdachte Veranda verbunden, die auf den Eingang des Grundstücks ausgerichtet ist. Die enge Beziehung des Gebäudes zu seiner Umgebung wird auch durch seine leichte und transparente Konstruktion unterstrichen, die weder die Natur noch die lokale Architektur dominiert. Das minimalistische Design wird durch die Verwendung von Glas, Holz und Stein hervorgehoben. Natürliche Materialien spielen eine besonders wichtige Rolle bei den Außenwänden und Böden, wo die Architekten lokalen „Serpentino"-Stein verwendet haben. Im Inneren harmonieren die Holzböden gut mit den warmen Farbtönen der Wände und Möbel. Das Ziel der Architekten war es, ein komfortables Haus zu schaffen, damit die Bewohner die Naturlandschaft genießen können. Verglaste Wände erfüllen das Haus mit Licht. Der teilweise überdachte und mit einem Swimmingpool ausgestattete Außenbereich schafft einen fließenden Übergang zwischen dem Inneren und dem Garten.

Construite sur un vaste terrain entouré de montagnes et de vignobles exceptionnels, la villa Geef fait la part belle aux paysages. La maison de plain-pied, clairement divisée en deux parties, est immergée dans son environnement naturel. Un côté du bâtiment est occupé par le garage et les pièces de réception, l'autre par la résidence du propriétaire. Tous deux sont reliés par un porche couvert aligné avec l'entrée du terrain. La relation étroite qu'entretient l'édifice avec son environnement est également soulignée par sa construction légère et transparente qui ne domine nullement la nature ni ne tranche avec l'architecture locale. Le design minimaliste est mis en relief par l'utilisation du verre, du bois et de la pierre. Les matériaux naturels jouent un rôle particulièrement important sur les murs extérieurs et les sols, où les architectes ont utilisé une pierre locale appelée «Serpentino». À l'intérieur, les sols en bois s'harmonisent bien avec les tons chauds des murs et du mobilier. L'objectif des architectes était de créer une maison confortable pour faire profiter les habitants du paysage naturel. De grandes baies vitrées emplissent la maison de lumière. L'espace construit à l'extérieur, en partie couvert et équipé d'une piscine, crée une transition fluide entre l'intérieur et le jardin.

ARCHITECTS: DAMILANOSTUDIO ARCHITECTS _ PROJECT LEADER DUILIO DAMILANO /// **COMPLETION:** 2017 /// **FURTHER PARTICIPANTS:** ARCHITECT ENRICO MASSIMINO /// **FLOOR AREA:** 750 M² (8,070 FT²) /// **PHOTOS:** ANDREA MARTIRADONNA

Façade opening up towards the garden and terrace view

Fassade an der Gartenseite und Blick auf die Terrasse

Façade côté jardin et vue sur la terrasse

Interiors Innenräume Intérieurs

Kitchen, living and dining area

Küche, Wohn- und Esszimmer

Cuisine, salon et salle à manger

Façade opening up towards the garden

Façade côté jardin

Fassade an der Gartenseite

FAMILY HOUSE "HEART"

HAVLÍČKŮV BROD, CZECH REPUBLIC

Family House "Heart" The name of this unique family house comes from the shape of the floor plan, which strongly evokes a heart. The organic form of the volume was largely inspired by the contours of the plot, which is not the only way the architects adjusted the residence to the local topography. Due to the sloping terrain with a significant difference between the top of the parcel and the street level, the house is built on two floors. The lower level includes the garage and utility rooms, and also the main access to the house. The top floor consists of the living area and, as it sits at the very top of the site, it opens through glazed walls onto the garden, in contrast to the entrance, where the closed façade has only a few windows. Sitting on the outdoor balcony, one can enjoy a picturesque view of the forest nearby. To create a visually harmonic space, the architects used natural materials and colours. The sophisticated curved walls crowned by the wooden beam pergola are the most striking elements in the structure.

Einfamilien Haus „Herz" Der Name dieses einzigartigen Einfamilienhauses kommt von seiner herzförmigen Konstruktion. Das organische Erscheinungsbild des Gebäudes wurde weitgehend durch die Konturen des Geländes bestimmt. Dies ist nicht das einzige Beispiel, das zeigt, wie die Architekten die Topographie ausnutzen konnten. Das abschüssige Gelände mit einem erheblichen Unterschied zwischen der Grundstücksspitze und dem Straßenniveau veranlasste die Architekten, das Haus auf zwei Etagen zu bauen. Im unteren Stockwerk befinden sich die Garage und die Wirtschaftsräume sowie der Hauptzugang zum Haus. Wohnräume befinden sich im Obergeschoss, und da es sich ganz oben auf dem Gelände befindet, fällt der Blick vom Wohnzimmer durch große Glaswände in den Garten. Diese Anordnung ist das Gegenteil von der für den Eingang entworfenen, deren geschlossene Fassade nur wenige Fenster beinhaltet. Von der Terrasse aus kann man den Ausblick auf den malerischen nahe gelegenen Wald genießen. Um eine gewisse Harmonie zwischen dem Haus und der Umgebung zu schaffen, verwendeten die Architekten natürliche Materialien und Farben. Die elegant gerundeten Wände, gekrönt von einer holzbalkenförmigen Pergola, sind die auffälligsten Merkmale des Gebäudes.

Maison familiale « Cœur » Le nom de cette maison familiale unique en son genre vient de sa construction en forme de cœur. L'aspect organique du bâtiment a été largement déterminé par les contours du terrain. Ce n'est pas d'ailleurs la seule caractéristique qui montre comment les architectes ont su tirer profits de la topographie. Le terrain en pente avec une différence importante entre le haut de la parcelle et le niveau de la rue a incité les architectes à construire la maison sur deux étages. L'étage inférieur comprend le garage et les pièces de service, ainsi que l'accès principal à la maison. La salle de séjour est à l'étage supérieur et, comme il se trouve tout en haut du site, la vue depuis le salon plonge sur le jardin à travers de larges baies vitrées. Cette disposition est à l'opposé de celle conçue pour l'entrée dont la façade fermée ne comporte que de rares fenêtres. Assis sur la terrasse, on peut admirer la vue pittoresque sur la forêt toute proche. Pour créer une certaine harmonie entre la maison et les alentours, les architectes ont utilisé des matériaux et des couleurs naturelles. Les murs délicatement arrondis et couronnés par une pergola en poutres de bois sont les éléments les plus marquants de l'édifice.

ARCHITECTS: DANIELA POLUBĚDOVOVÁ /// **COMPLETION:** 2017 /// **FURTHER PARTICIPANTS:** ING. JIŘÍ VÁCLAVŮ, ING PETR JANČÍK, MILAN BULVA /// **FLOOR AREA:** 241 M² (2,600 FT²) /// **PHOTOS:** FILIP ŠLAPAL

Entrance Eingangsbereich Entrée

Exterior view Außenansicht Vue extérieure

Ground floor plan

Grundriss Erdgeschoss

Plan du rez-de-chaussée

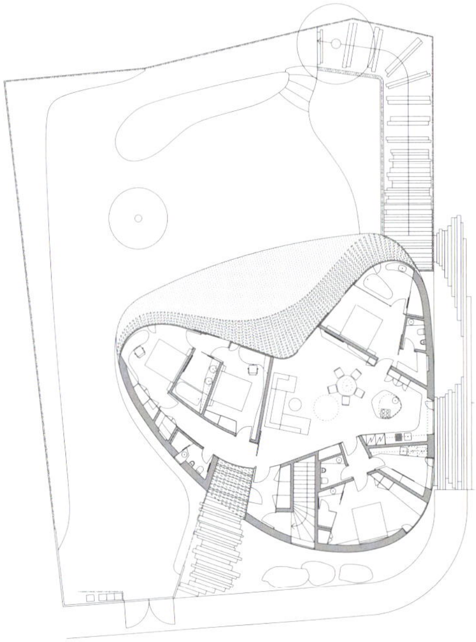

Interiors Innenraum Intérieur

ARCHITECTS: DAVIDE MACULLO ARCHITECTS /// **COMPLETION:** 2017 /// **FURTHER PARTICIPANTS:** LORENZA TALLARINI, MICHELE ALBERIO /// **FLOOR AREA:** 857 M² (9,225 FT²) /// **PHOTOS:** ALEXANDRE ZVEIGER

Street façade

Fassade an der Straßenseite

Façade côté rue

Façade opening up towards the garden

Fassade an der Gartenseite

Façade côté jardin

SWISS HOUSE XXXIV

GALBISIO, SWITZERLAND

Swiss House XXXIV, located in a mountainous setting, is eye-catching with its massive and complex structure that looks different depending on one's perspective as well as on the time of day. At night, when illuminated from inside, it creates an even more impressive effect. As a marker in the landscape, the house also echoes the forms of the surrounding nature. The architects' ultimate goal was to provide comfort to the inhabitants, so they envisioned a protective volume enclosed by a set of concrete slabs. Starting as a cube and based on a square plan, extensive blades have been shifted three dimensionally to maintain privacy and to also open the interiors to the Alpine landscape. The sharp angles and wide planes are what define this multifaceted construction, adhered to the gently sloping plot. The interiors are just as complex and offer a dynamic space arrangement. The stark opposition between breathing in the surrounding views and the massive construction creates an interesting contrast, just like the juxtaposition of concrete and glass in the façades.

Das in einer bergigen Umgebung liegende Schweizer Haus XXXIV, beeindruckt durch seine massive und komplexe Struktur, die je nach Blickwinkel und Tageszeit im Aussehen variiert. Nachts, von innen beleuchtet, ist sein Aussehen noch faszinierender. Das Haus tritt wie ein Wahrzeichen aus der Landschaft hervor, spiegelt jedoch gleichzeitig die Formensprache seiner Umgebung wieder. Um den Bewohnern maximalen Komfort zu bieten, haben sich die Architekten ein riesiges Gebäude vorgestellt, das von großen schützenden Betonplatten umgeben ist. Diese großen Platten wurden würfelförmig rund um die Villa angebracht, um die Privatsphäre des Gebäudes zu wahren, ohne den Bewohnern den Blick auf die schöne alpine Landschaft zu nehmen. Scharfe Winkel und weite Ebenen definieren diese facettenreiche Konstruktion, die sich an ein sanft abfallendes Grundstück schmiegt. Die Innenräume sind ebenso aufwendig und bieten eine dynamische Raumgestaltung. Der große Gegensatz zwischen dem Eindruck von endlosem Raum, der durch die umgebende Landschaft entsteht, und der massiven Konstruktion, die das Land abgrenzt, sowie das Nebeneinander von Beton und Glas an den Fassaden bilden einen markanten Kontrast.

La Maison Suisse XXXIV, située dans un cadre montagneux, impressionne par sa structure massive et complexe qui prend un air différent selon l'emplacement d'où on la regarde et selon l'heure de la journée. La nuit, éclairée de l'intérieur, son aspect est encore plus fascinant. La maison est un point de repère dans le paysage même si elle reproduit les formes escarpées qui l'environnent. Pour offrir un maximum de confort aux habitants, les architectes ont imaginé un vaste bâtiment entouré des grands panneaux protecteurs en béton. Disposées en forme de cube, ces grandes dalles ont été placées tout autour de la villa pour en préserver l'intimité sans pour autant priver les habitants des superbes paysages alpins. Les angles aigus et les plans larges définissent cette construction aux facettes multiples, accrochée à une parcelle en pente douce. Les intérieurs sont tout aussi élaborés et offrent un aménagement dynamique de l'espace. Le contraste très fort entre l'impression d'espace sans fin que procure le paysage environnant et la construction massive qui délimite le terrain crée un contraste saisissant, tout comme la juxtaposition du béton et du verre sur les façades.

Exterior view Außenansicht Vue extérieure

Terrace view

Blick auf die Terrasse

Vue sur la terrasse

Interior view Innenansicht Vue intérieure

HOUSE KERK-STRAAT

BEEK EN DONK, THE NETHERLANDS

"One house, five different volumes" would be the most concise way to describe this fragmented residence. The brickwork façade from the street side, with narrow tall windows, absorbs traffic noise and creates a visual barrier, "hiding" the structure which evolves toward the garden on the back of the plot. Spaces are accommodated in both individual and linked volumes. The front part houses the living areas and office. The kitchen is located in the wooden volume behind and has folding doors towards the outdoor sitting area. The dining space in the third part of the complex, also in brickwork, is defined by its narrow and tall windows on the upper level and big openings on the ground floor. While the garage is situated in a dark wooden part, the last and separate volume offers space to relax, connected to a terrace and a pool facing the back garden. The pitched roofs are the only element in common across all structures, which are diverse in size and shape. Through the whole complex, a good balance is maintained between intimacy and a fluid connection with the surroundings.

„Ein Haus, fünf verschiedene Gebäude" ist wohl die kürzeste Art, dieses in fünf Teile geteilte Wohnhaus zu beschreiben. Die Ziegelfassade an der Straßenseite mit hohen, schmalen Fenstern absorbiert den Verkehrslärm und bildet eine optische Barriere, die die gartenseitigen Gebäude auf der Rückseite des Grundstücks abschirmt. Die Räume sind sowohl als voneinander unabhängige Gebäude angeordnet als auch als einzelner zusammenhängender Baukörper konzipiert. Der vordere Teil beherbergt die Wohn- und Büroräume. Die Küche befindet sich in einem Holzgebäude gleich dahinter und hat Schiebetüren zum Außensitzbereich. Das im dritten, in Ziegelmauerwerk errichteten Gebäudekomplex gelegene Esszimmer zeichnet sich durch seine schmalen, hohen Fenster im Obergeschoss und große Öffnungen im Erdgeschoss aus. Während die Garage in einem dunklen Holzbauteil installiert ist, bietet das letzte, von den anderen Gebäuden getrennte Bauwerk einen Entspannungsbereich, der mit einer Terrasse und einem Swimmingpool mit Blick auf den hinteren Teil des Gartens verbunden ist. Die Satteldächer sind das einzige Element, das allen Strukturen, die in Größe und Form variieren, gemeinsam ist. Im gesamten Ensemble wird ein Gleichgewicht zwischen der Rücksicht auf die Privatsphäre. Das gesamt Ensemble wahrt das Gleichgewicht zwischen der Rücksicht auf die Privatsphäre und einer fließenden Verbindung mit der Umgebung.

« Une maison, cinq bâtiments différents » est sans doute la façon la plus concise de décrire cette résidence fragmentée en cinq parties. La façade en brique, côté rue, avec de hautes fenêtres étroites, absorbe les bruits de la circulation et crée une barrière visuelle qui cache les constructions côté jardin à l'arrière de la parcelle. Les espaces sont aménagés à la fois comme des bâtiments individuels et comme des éléments reliés entre eux. La partie avant abrite les pièces de séjour et les bureaux. La cuisine est située dans un bâtiment en bois juste derrière et dispose des portes coulissantes vers le salon extérieur. Située dans la troisième partie du complexe, qui est en maçonnerie, la salle à manger est caractérisée par ses fenêtres étroites et hautes à l'étage supérieur et ses grandes ouvertures au rez-de-chaussée. Alors que le garage est installé dans une partie en bois sombre, le dernier bâtiment, séparé des autres, offre un espace de détente relié à une terrasse et à une piscine donnant sur le fond du jardin. Les toits en pente sont le seul élément commun à toutes les structures qui varient en taille et en forme. Tout au long de l'ensemble, l'équilibre est maintenu entre souci d'intimité et d'harmonie avec l'environnement naturel.

ARCHITECTS: DENKKAMER ARCHITECTUUR /// **COMPLETION:** 2018 /// **FLOOR AREA:** 358 M² (3,850 FT²) /// **PHOTOS:** STIJN POELSTRA, JEROEN KUPPENS

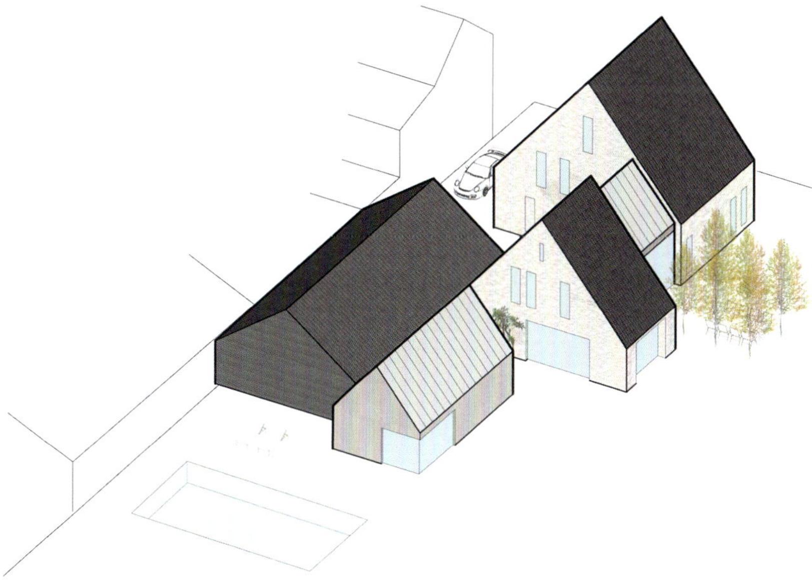

Axonometry

Axonometrie

Vue axonométrique

Street façade

Fassade an der Straßenseite

Façade côté rue

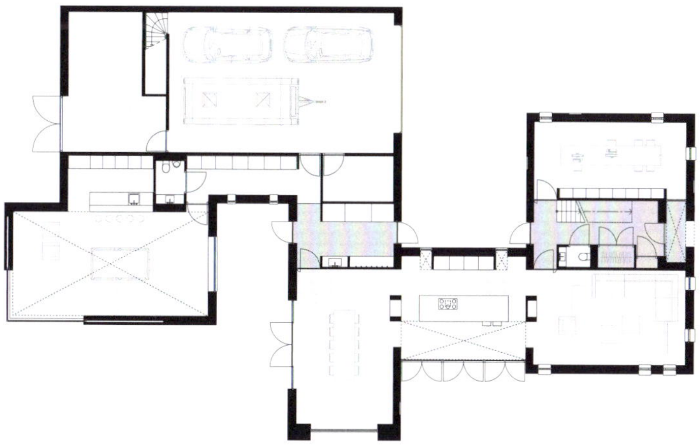

Patio

Pool house Swimmingpool Piscine

Entrance hall Eingangshalle Hall d'entrée

Ground floor plan

Grundriss Erdgeschoss

Plan du rez-de-chaussée

ARCHITECTS: FUCHS, WACKER. ARCHITEKTEN BDA /// **COMPLETION:** 2016 /// **FLOOR AREA:** 440 M² (4,735 FT²) ///
PHOTOS: JOHANNES VOGT

Section Schnitt Section

Exterior view Außenansicht Vue extérieure

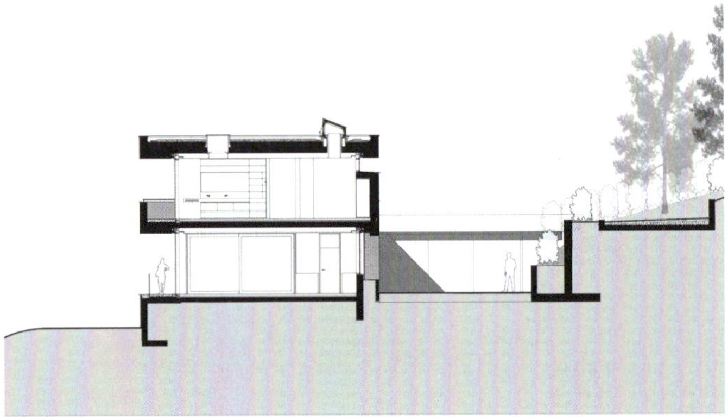

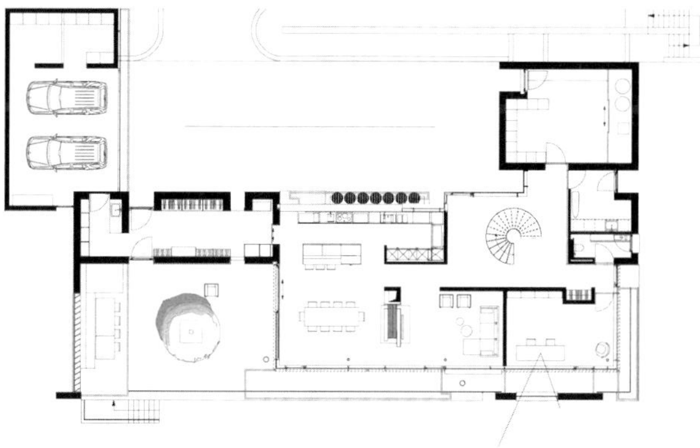

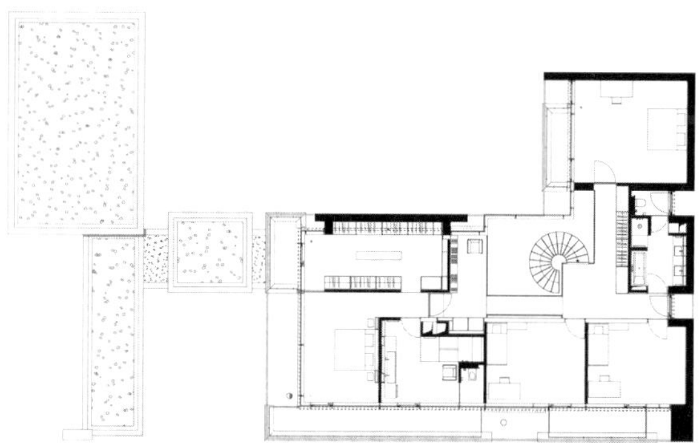

HOUSE FMB

ESSLINGEN, GERMANY

The architects designed this house according to two main wishes from the owners. As it is a family residence, the first goal was to create enough space for children to play. The second considered the building's relation to the context – it needed to respect rather than dominate the landscape. The elegant and harmonious structure, though extensive, nestles into the southern slope. While the top floor is visible from the street level, the lower blends into the garden. The balanced and transparent volume offers inhabitants ample space both inside and outside, including a place to play football, and to enjoy their everyday family life. The clear lines enhanced by classic materials and colours are complemented by a warm interior design. The minimalistic character of the space is punctuated up by highlights such as a ribbon-like staircase. As the plot is located above the city centre, the owners can enjoy amazing views of the valley, forest, or mountains or decide to draw the curtains on panoramic windows and create a cosy atmosphere inside. Apart from the entrance façade, all other elevations remain open to the surroundings.

Die Grundlage für den Entwurf diese Hauses bildeten zwei Wünsche des Bauherren. Da es sich um ein Familienhaus handelt, war der erste Wunsch, genügend Platz zum Spielen für die Kinder zu schaffen. Der zweite betraf die Beziehung zwischen dem Gebäude und seiner Umgebung; es sollte die Landschaft nicht dominieren, sondern respektieren. Trotz seiner Ausdehnung schmiegt sich das elegante und harmonische Gebäude an den Südhang eines Hügels. Während die Silhouette des obersten Stockwerks von der Straße aus sichtbar ist, fügt sich der Rest des Gebäudes in den Garten ein. Das gut proportionierte und transparente Gebäude bietet den Bewohnern einen großen bietet seinen Bewohnern einen Innen- und Außenbereich mit reichlich Platz für das Familienleben, sogar für Fußballspielen. Klassische Materialien und Farben heben die klaren Linien hervor und werden durch die warme Inneneinrichtung ergänzt. Der minimalistische Charakter des Raumes wird durch Highlights wie eine bandförmige Treppe unterstrichen. Das oberhalb des Zentrums von Essligen gelegene Anwesen erlaubt den Eigentümern, die atemberaubende Aussicht auf das Tal, den Wald oder die Berge zu bewundern. Wenn sie sich entscheiden, die Vorhänge an den Panoramafenstern zu schliessen, schaffen sie im Inneren eine warme und intime Atmosphäre. Mit Ausnahme der Eingangsfassade zeigen sich alle anderen Ansichten zur Umgebung hin offen.

Les architectes ont conçu cette maison en tenant compte de deux souhaits exprimés par les propriétaires. Comme il s'agit d'une résidence familiale, le premier souhait était de créer suffisamment d'espace pour que les enfants puissent jouer. Le second touchait la relation entre le bâtiment et son environnement ; il devait respecter le paysage plutôt que le dominer. Bien qu'étendu, l'édifice élégant et harmonieux se niche sur le versant sud d'une colline. Si la silhouette du dernier étage est visible depuis la rue, le reste se fond dans le jardin. Le bâtiment bien proportionné et transparent offre aux habitants un grand espace intérieur et extérieur, avec même un endroit pour jouer au football, et semble idéalement conçu pour profiter de la vie de famille au quotidien. Les lignes claires mises en valeur par des matériaux et des couleurs classiques sont complétées par une décoration intérieure chaleureuse. Le caractère minimaliste de l'espace est ponctué par des points forts tels qu'un escalier en forme de ruban. Le terrain, situé au-dessus du centre-ville d'Essligen, permet aux propriétaires d'admirer la vue imprenable sur la vallée, la forêt ou les montagnes. S'ils décident de tirer les rideaux des fenêtres panoramiques, ils créent alors une atmosphère chaleureuse et intimiste à l'intérieur. À l'exception de la façade d'entrée, toutes les autres élévations restent ouvertes sur l'espace environnant.

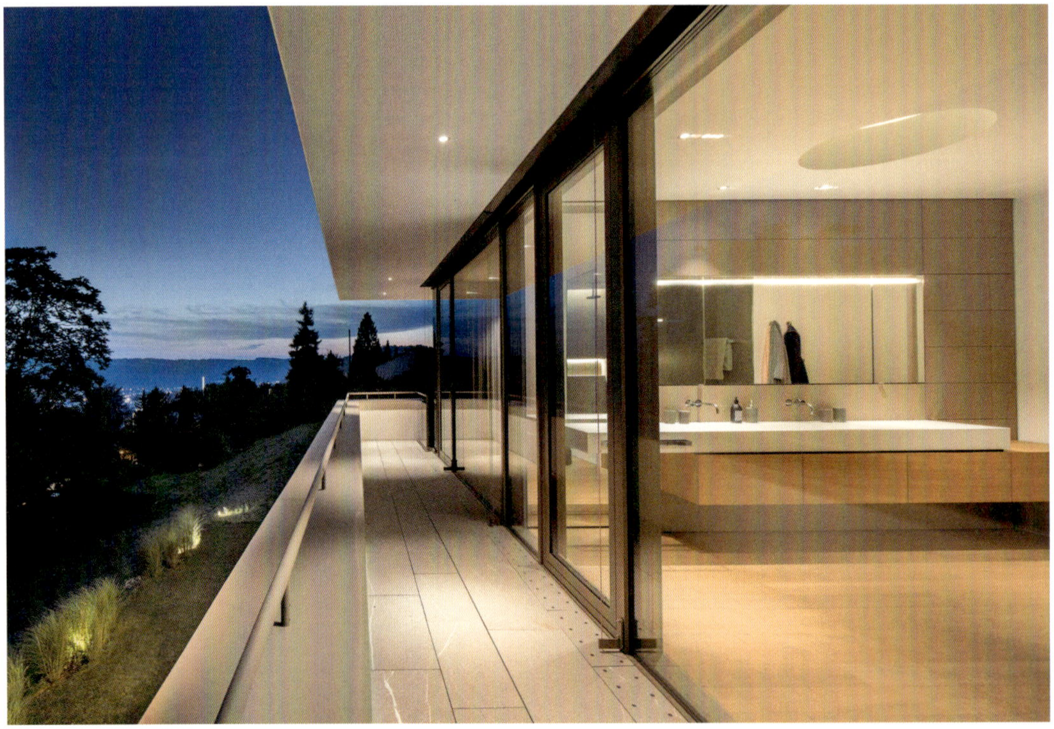

Terrace view

Blick auf die Terrasse

Vue sur la terrasse

Interior Innenraum Intérieur

MEHRGE-NERATIO-NENHAUS

TEUFENTHAL, SWITZERLAND

Designed as a multi-generational home (the main single-family house is connected to an additional small flat), the building is eye-catching with its purity of geometric forms. The solidity of the cubic volume is broken up by square openings in various sizes, placed irregularly on all façades. In addition, a terrace cut out from one of the corners of the top floor repeats the same square form. Its modern look and the lack of a pitched roof, so characteristic of neighbouring houses, makes it stand out from the context. Nevertheless, thanks to the grey colour of the exterior walls and well-balanced proportions, the house blends into the landscape. The interiors are minimalistic, clear, and very practical. Numerous windows, in particular two extensive terrace openings, bordering the staircase running from the basement to the top floor, distribute plenty of natural light within the house. The access to light as well as wooden windows and parts of the interior fittings all serve to soften the massive character of the concrete walls and ceilings. The grandparents' flat occupies the ground floor together with the children's area and a multipurpose room, while the top floor fits the parents' room, living and dining areas, and the terrace.

Das Gebäude, das mehrere Generationen unter einem Dach beherbergt (zu diesem umfangreichen Familienwohnsitz gehört auch eine kleine separate Wohnung), besticht durch die Reinheit seiner geometrischen Formen. Das brutalistische kubische Erscheinungsbild wird durch quadratische Fenster unterschiedlicher Größe aufgeweicht, die unregelmäßig an allen Fassaden platziert sind. Darüber hinaus nimmt eine in eine der Ecken des Obergeschosses geschnitzte Terrasse die gleiche quadratische Form an. Das moderne Design des Gebäudes und das Fehlen des für die Nachbarhäuser so charakteristischen Schrägdachs unterscheiden die Villa von anderen Wohnhäusern in der Umgebung. Dennoch fügt sich das Haus dank der grauen Farbe der Außenwände und seiner ausgewogenen Proportionen gut in die Landschaft ein. Die Innenräume sind minimalistisch, leicht und sehr praktisch. Die Fenster, insbesondere die beiden großen zur Terrasse, die die Treppe vom Keller zum ersten Stockwerk säumen, sorgen für viel natürliches Licht. Das hohe Maß an Licht, die Holzfenster und einige Elemente der Innenarchitektur dienen dazu, den massiven Charakter der Betonwände und -decken zu mildern. Die Wohnung der Großeltern sowie die Kinderzimmer und ein Mehrzweckraum nehmen das Erdgeschoss ein, während im Obergeschoss das Elternschlafzimmer, das Wohnzimmer, das Esszimmer und die Terrasse untergebracht sind.

Destiné à accueillir plusieurs générations sous un même toit (cette vaste résidence familiale comprend aussi un petit appartement à part), le bâtiment attire le regard par la pureté de ses formes géométriques. L'aspect cubique brutaliste est adouci par des fenêtres carrées de tailles variables et placées de façon irrégulière sur toutes les façades. En outre, une terrasse taillée dans l'un des angles du dernier étage reprend la même forme carrée. L'allure moderne de la construction et l'absence de toit en pente si caractéristique des maisons voisines distinguent la villa des autres habitations aux alentours. Néanmoins, grâce à la couleur grise des murs extérieurs et à ses proportions bien équilibrées, la maison s'intègre bien dans le paysage. Les intérieurs sont minimalistes, clairs et très pratiques. Les fenêtres, notamment les deux grandes baies vitrées sur la terrasse et qui bordent l'escalier allant du sous-sol au premier étage, procurent beaucoup de lumière naturelle. La grande luminosité, des fenêtres en bois et certains éléments de l'aménagement intérieur servent à adoucir le caractère massif des murs et des plafonds en béton. L'appartement des grands-parents occupe le rez-de-chaussée ainsi que les chambres des enfants et une salle polyvalente, tandis que l'étage supérieur accueille la chambre des parents, le salon, la salle à manger et la terrasse.

ARCHITECTS: GAUTSCHI LENZIN SCHENKER ARCHITEKTEN AG /// **COMPLETION:** 2018 /// **FURTHER PARTICIPANTS:** KONSTRUKTIV GMBH INGENIEURE UND PLANER, GÄNICHEN /// **FLOOR AREA:** 245 M² (2,640 FT²) /// **PHOTOS:** ANDREAS GRABER PHOTOGRAPHY

Exterior view Außenansicht Vue extérieure

Ground floor interiors

Innenräume Erdgeschoss

Intérieurs (rez-de-chaussée)

First floor interiors

Innenräume Obergeschoss

Intérieurs (premier étage)

ARCHITECTS: GRAFT GMBH /// **COMPLETION:** 2017 /// **FURTHER PARTICIPANTS:** BÜRO HAPPOLD, BERLIN (STRUCTURAL AND TECHNICAL PLANNING), KRE_TA, BERLIN (LANDSCAPE ARCHITECT), MÜLLER BBM, BERLIN (BUILDING PHYSICS), HHP, BERLIN (FIRE SAFETY), IABU – PRENZEL & PARTNER, BERLIN (CDM CO-ORDINATOR), BARTELS VERMESSUNG, BERLIN (GAUGER) /// **FLOOR AREA:** 530 M^2 (5,700 FT^2) /// **PHOTOS:** TOBIAS HEIN (EXTERIOR), FRANK HERFORT (INTERIOR)

Street façade

Fassade an der Straßenseite

Façade côté rue

VILLA M

BERLIN GRUNEWALD, GERMANY

Sitting in the middle of a residential area on the outskirts of the German capital, Villa M is visually striking with its sculptural and distinctive form. The architects designed a trapezoidal volume by abstracting the classical rules of villa design and synthetizing them digitally, with natural phenomena shifting the tectonics. Symbolizing a boulder in a glacial landscape, the house is clad with ceramic plates which enhance the stone-like effect. Arranged on four levels, one of which connects the street with the garden level, the multifaceted façades juxtapose edgy walls with numerous openings. Loggias and floor-to-ceiling windows provide both connections with the surroundings and privacy at the same time. The fluidly designed interiors are spacious and comfortable, with a living room on the ground floor as the heart of the house. The top level is designed as a self-contained flat; however, each floor can be transformed into an individual apartment with a staircase providing easy access. As the floor plans are envisioned in a very flexible way, the house can be easily adjusted to the owners' needs.

Mitten in einem Wohngebiet am Rande der deutschen Hauptstadt gelegen, fasziniert die Villa M durch ihre skulpturale und unverwechselbare Form. Den Architekten gelang es, ein trapezförmiges Gebäude zu bauen, indem sie die klassischen Regeln des Villendesigns modellierten und die Naturphänomene, die die Tektonik beeinflussen, digital synthetisierten. Das Haus, das einen Felsen in einer Gletscherlandschaft darstellt, ist mit Keramikplatten verkleidet, die den Eindruck einer Steinoberfläche verstärken. Die viergeschossige Villa, von denen eines als Verbindung zwischen Straßenzugang und Garten dient, hat mehrkantige Fassaden mit eckigen Wänden und Erkern. Loggien und raumhohe Fenster verbinden den Außen- und Innenraum miteinander und wahren gleichzeitig die Privatsphäre. Die Innenräume sind mit dem Wunsch nach fließendem Design, Raum und Komfort gestaltet. Ein Wohnzimmer im Erdgeschoss ist das Herzstück des Hauses. Das Obergeschoss ist als eigenständiges Appartement ausgelegt; jedes Stockwerk kann jedoch in ein individuelles Appartement mit einer Treppe für den einfachen Zugang umgewandelt werden. Da die Raumaufteilung sehr flexibel ist, kann das Haus leicht an die Bedürfnisse der Eigentümer angepasst werden.

Située au milieu d'un quartier résidentiel à la périphérie de la capitale allemande, la Villa M intrigue par sa forme sculpturale et distinctive. Les architectes ont réussi à construire un bâtiment trapézoïdal en modélisant les règles classiques de la conception des villas et en synthétisant numériquement les phénomènes naturels qui influent sur la tectonique. La maison qui représente un rocher dans un paysage glaciaire, est revêtue de plaques de céramique qui renforcent l'impression d'une surface en pierre. La villa de quatre étages, dont l'un sert à relier l'accès rue au jardin, présente des façades aux arêtes multiples où se succèdent murs anguleux et baies vitrées. Les loggias et les fenêtres allant du sol au plafond facilitent le passage de l'intérieur vers l'extérieur tout en protégeant l'intimité. Les intérieurs sont conçus dans un désir de fluidité, d'espace et de confort. Un salon au rez-de-chaussée constitue le cœur de la maison. L'étage supérieur est conçu comme un appartement indépendant ; toutefois, chaque étage peut être transformé en un appartement individuel avec un escalier permettant un accès facile. Comme les plans sont conçus de manière très flexible, la maison peut être facilement adaptée aux besoins des propriétaires.

Façade opening up towards the garden

Fassade an der Gartenseite

Façade côté jardin

Interiors Innenräume Intérieurs

ARCHITECTS: GEORG DÖRING ARCHITEKTEN BDA /// **COMPLETION:** 2016 /// **FLOOR AREA:** 316 M² (3,400 FT²) ///
PHOTOS: MICHAEL REISCH

Street façade

Fassade an der Straßenseite

Façade côté rue

Entrance Eingangsbereich Entrée

NEUBAU EINFAMILIENHAUS

MÜLHEIM AN DER RUHR, GERMANY

The plot, both narrow and deep, on a very busy road created a challenge for this two-storey single-family house. The spacious interiors, encompassing eight rooms, a kitchen, and bathrooms, are wrapped in a rather massive outer shell covered with brickwork. While the side elevations of the house are quite regular, the architects played with the entrance and garden façade. The first one forms a stark contrast between the solid top volume and the extensive glazed entrance hall. On the opposite side, large floor-to-ceiling windows connect the ground floor with the garden, and the top floor opens over it with a terrace running along nearly the whole length of the house. What looks heavy and solid from the street perspective (and also serves to block street noise) becomes far lighter and transparent in the back. To save space, the garage was placed underground. Both floors were planned as open and flowing spaces. The compact cube gives the owners privacy and allows them to benefit from an outside seating area and garden, separated from the busy road.

Das enge und steile Grundstück, das an einer viel befahrenen Straße liegt, stellte eine Herausforderung für den Bau dieses zweistöckigen Einfamilienhauses dar. Die großen Innenräume umfassen acht Zimmer, eine Küche und mehrere Badezimmer. Sie sind in einen ziemlich massiven, mit Ziegelsteinen bedeckten Außenmantel gehüllt. Während die Seitenansichten des Hauses eher unauffällig gestaltet wurden, haben die Architekten mit den Volumen an den Eingangs- und Gartenfassaden gespielt. Erstere ist durch den markanten Kontrast zwischen dem einteiligen Block im Obergeschoss und der großen verglasten Eingangshalle im Erdgeschoss gekennzeichnet. Auf der gegenüberliegenden Seite verbinden große, raumhohe Fenster das Erdgeschoss mit dem Garten, und das Obergeschoss öffnet sich zum Garten hin mit einer Terrasse, die sich fast über die gesamte Länge des Hauses erstreckt. Was an der Straßenseite schwer und kompakt erscheint, vor allem aber der Abschirmung des Straßenlärms dient, wird im hinteren Bereich viel leichter und transparent. Um Platz zu sparen, wurde die Garage unterirdisch installiert. Beide Etagen wurden als offene, fließende Räume gestaltet. Die Form des kompakten Kubushauses gibt den Eigentümern eine gewisse Privatsphäre und ermöglicht es ihnen, von einem Sitzplatz im Freien und einem von der verkehrsreichen Straße abgetrennten Garten zu profitieren.

Le terrain, à la fois étroit et escarpé, qui plus est situé sur une route très fréquentée, a constitué un défi pour la construction de cette maison individuelle de deux étages. Les intérieurs spacieux comprennent huit pièces, une cuisine et des salles de bain. Ils sont enveloppés dans une coque extérieure plutôt massive recouverte de briques. Si les élévations latérales de la maison sont assez régulières, les architectes ont en revanche joué avec les volumes sur la façade de l'entrée et sur celle du jardin. La première est marquée par le contraste saisissant entre l'étage supérieur en un seul bloc et le vaste hall d'entrée vitré au rez-de-chaussée. Sur le côté opposé, de grandes fenêtres du sol au plafond relient le rez-de-chaussée au jardin, et l'étage supérieur s'ouvre sur celui-ci avec une terrasse qui s'étend sur presque toute la longueur de la maison. Ce qui semble lourd et compact côté rue (mais sert surtout à bloquer les bruits de la route) devient beaucoup plus léger et transparent à l'arrière. Pour gagner de l'espace, le garage a été installé sous terre. Les deux étages ont été conçus comme des espaces ouverts et fluides. La forme de la maison en cube compact donne aux propriétaires une certaine intimité et leur permet de bénéficier d'un espace extérieur pour s'asseoir et d'un jardin séparé de la route très fréquentée.

Interiors Innenräume Intérieurs

Terrace view

Blick auf die Terrasse

Vue sur la terrasse

Basement, ground and first floor plans

Grundrisse Untergeschoss, Erdgeschoss und Obergeschosses

Plans du sous-sol, du rez-de-chaussée et du premier étage

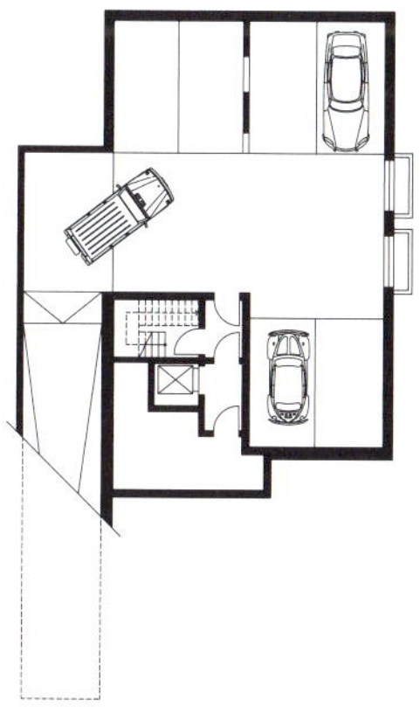

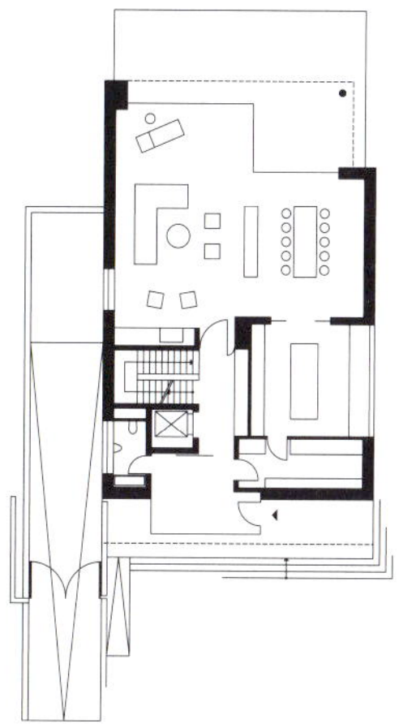

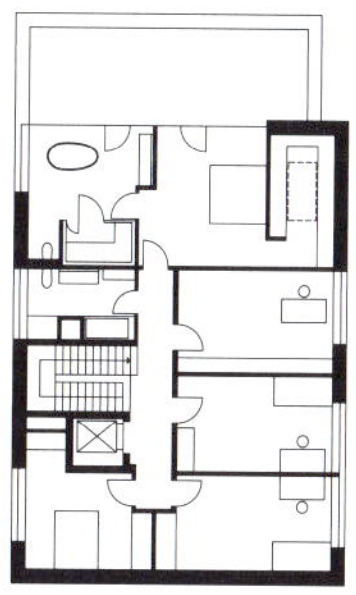

HAUS AM ALBTRAUF

NEUFFEN, GERMANY

The power of this villa is in its purely minimalistic shape, particularly striking due to its large scale. The three floors covered with a pitched roof are a reference to the simplest form of a house, expressed here, however, in a more modern language. Built into a slope, the villa presents itself completely differently from all four perspectives. As the western gable façade faces a beautiful view of the valley, all the levels have been fully glazed and have balconies along the whole width of the house. This solution not only allows the owners to enjoy the panorama but also gives the monolithic volume some lightness. The western façade of the house is easily accessible from the street (with no fence bordering the plot), while the south elevation, with the entrance to the garage on the ground floor and a swimming pool above, creates a more intimate area. The outdoor space is connected with the heart of the house - the kitchen and dining area and the living room are divided by a cubic fireplace and a two-step level difference to create a fluid and spacious interior.

Der Zauber dieser Villa liegt in ihrer minimalistischen Form, die durch die außergewöhnliche Größe des Gebäudes besonders hervorgehoben wird. Die drei von einem Satteldach bedeckten Stockwerke beziehen sich auf die Grundstruktur eines traditionellen Hauses, doch wird sie hier im Sinne einer modernen Foremensprache überarbeitet. An einem Hang erbaut, präsentiert sich die Villa auf jeder Seite ganz anders. Da die giebelförmige Westfassade eine schöne Aussicht auf das Tal bietet, sind alle Stockwerke voll verglast und haben Balkone über die gesamte Breite des Hauses. Diese Lösung ermöglicht es den Eigentümern, das Panorama in vollem Umfang zu genießen; sie verleiht diesem monolithischen Gebäude auch eine gewisse Leichtigkeit. Während die Westseite des Hauses von der Straße aus leicht zugänglich ist (es gibt keine Zäune, die das Grundstück begrenzen), ist die Südseite, die vor Sicht geschützt ist, mit einem über der Garage installierten Swimmingpool ausgestattet. Diese Fassade verbindet das Haus auch mit dem Garten. Küche, Ess- und Wohnzimmer sind durch einen kubisch geformten Kamin und durch einen zweistufigen Höhenunterschied getrennt, um einen fließenden und geräumigen Innenraum zu schaffen.

La magie de cette villa réside dans sa forme minimaliste qui est particulièrement mise en avant par la dimension exceptionnelle du bâtiment. Les trois étages recouverts d'un toit en pente font référence à la structure élémentaire d'une maison traditionnelle, mais cette structure est retravaillée ici dans l'esprit de l'esthétique moderne. Construite en pente, la villa se présente de manière totalement différente de chaque côté. Comme la façade ouest, à pignon, offre une belle vue sur la vallée, tous les étages y sont entièrement vitrés et disposent de balcons sur toute la largeur de la maison. Cette solution permet aux propriétaires de profiter pleinement du panorama ; elle confère aussi une certaine légèreté à ce bâtiment monolithique. Si la façade ouest de la maison est facilement accessible depuis la rue (aucune clôture ne borde le terrain), la façade sud, protégée des regards, est équipée d'une piscine installée au-dessus du garage. Cette façade relie également la maison au jardin. La cuisine, la salle à manger et le salon sont séparés par une cheminée cubique et par une différence de niveau de deux marches pour créer un intérieur fluide et spacieux.

East façade Ostfassade Façade est

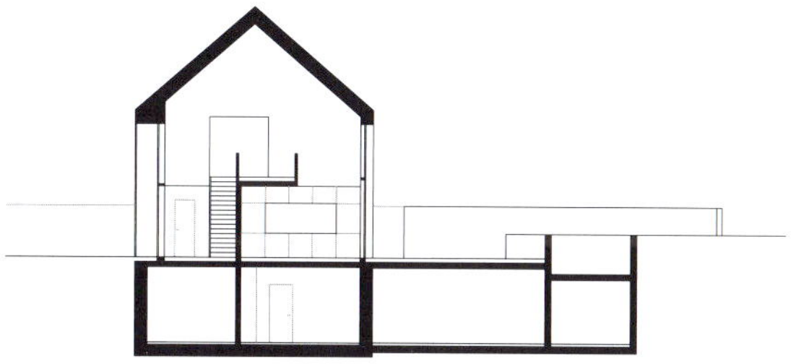

West façade Westfassade Façade ouest

North façade Nordfassade Façade nord

Section Schnitt Section

ARCHITECTS: HENRIK ISERMANN – HI ARCHITEKTUR /// **COMPLETION:** 2017 /// **FLOOR AREA:** 250 M² (2,690 FT²) ///
PHOTOS FOTOS PHOTOS: JÜRGEN POLLAK

Interiors Innenräume Intérieurs

HOUSE L-C

ANZEGEM, BELGIUM

Located on a charming village road, this house takes an original zig-zaging shape. The architects, challenged by the trapezium shape of the plot, envisioned this interesting concept to create a semi-open house. The street façade is narrow and evolves toward the back garden of the side. As the house occupies a corner, the site elevation also becomes part of the street view. It is further developed in a zig-zag manner to make the side garden a full addendum to the house and not just a driveway. The curious building consists of three cubes with varying roof heights. While the front and side parts are two floors high, the back façade has only one level and is largely glazed to create a soft connection between the interiors and a grassy area, intimately hidden at the far end of the plot. Each rectangular volume fits a different function including an office, a dining room, and a living room, all of which are connected at the point of their corners. The unusual structural arrangement creates visually interesting relations with the adjacent villa.

An einer reizvollen Dorfstraße gelegen, zeichnet sich dieses Haus durch seine außergewöhnliche Zickzackform aus. Angesichts der trapezförmigen Form des Grundstücks entwickelten die Architekten das außergewöhnliche Konzept eines halb freistehenden Hauses. Die Fassade an der Straßenseite ist schmal und weicht dem Weg, der zum Garten an der Rückseite des Hauses führt. Da das Gebäude an einer Straßenecke steht, ist ist diese Fassade auch von der Straße aus sichtbar. Das Haus ist in einem Zickzackmuster gebaut, um den Seitengarten zu einem integralen Bestandteil des Ensembles zu machen und nicht nur eine Zufahrt. Die Struktur der Villa besteht aus drei unterschiedlich hohen Kuben. Während der vordere und der mittlere Teil zwei Stockwerke hoch sind, ist die hintere Fassade nur ein Stockwerk hoch und weitgehend verglast, um einen fließenden Übergang zwischen den Innenräumen und einer Grasfläche zu schaffen, die am Ende des Grundstücks diskret verborgen ist. Jeder der drei Kuben, aus denen das Haus besteht, erfüllt eine andere Funktion: in einem ist ein Büro, im anderen ein Esszimmer und im dritten ein Wohnzimmer untergebracht. Alle diese Räume sind durch eine ihrer Ecken miteinander verbunden. Die ungewöhnliche bauliche Anordnung schafft eine sehr interessante visuelle Interaktion mit der angrenzenden Villa.

Située sur une charmante route de village, cette maison se caractérise par sa forme originale en zigzag. Les architectes, confrontés à la forme trapézoïdale du terrain, ont imaginé ce concept intéressant pour créer une maison semi-détachée. La façade côté rue est étroite et laisse place au chemin qui mène au jardin situé à l'arrière de la maison. Comme le bâtiment occupe un coin de rue, l'élévation latérale est également visible depuis la rue. La maison est construite en zigzag pour faire du jardin latéral un élément à part entière de l'aménagement et non une simple allée. La structure de la villa se compose de trois cubes dont la hauteur sous toit varie. Alors que les parties avant et médianes sont sur deux étages, la façade arrière n'en a qu'un et elle est largement vitrée pour créer une douce transition entre les intérieurs et une zone gazonnée, discrètement cachée à l'extrémité du terrain. Chacun des trois cubes qui composent la maison remplit une fonction différente :
l'un abrite un bureau, l'autre une salle à manger et le troisième un salon. Toutes ces pièces sont reliées par l'un de leurs angles. La disposition structurelle insolite crée une interaction visuelle très intéressante avec la villa adjacente.

ARCHITECTS: GRAUX & BAEYENS ARCHITECTEN /// **COMPLETION:** 2017 /// **FLOOR AREA:** 150 M² (1,614 FT²) ///
PHOTOS: JEROEN VERRECHT

Side façade

Seitenfassade

Façade latérale

Façade opening up towards the garden

Façade côté jardin

Fassade an der Gartenseite

Interiors Innenräume Intérieurs

ARCHITECTS: HPA + ARCHITEKTUR /// **COMPLETION:** 2018 /// **FURTHER PARTICIPANTS:** KUNSTLICHT E.K. /// **FLOOR AREA:** 250 M² (2,690 FT²) /// **PHOTOS:** HPA

HOUSE RMP HH

COLOGNE, GERMANY

Its long and narrow plot inspired this curious combination of a strong rectangular frame covered by a pitched roof and entirely glazed gable sides. The contrast of massiveness and transparency in this clear structure is visually strong as the house is three storeys high. The basement protrudes partly out of the ground. On the garden façade, it is entirely closed and looks like a plinth. The lowest level, which encompasses an individual flat, is not devoid of natural light, however, thanks to windows on the opposite elevation. The entire house is bright and furnished unobtrusively to offer owners comfortable and spacious interiors. Even the staircase between the floors is made of light construction, which becomes semi-transparent on higher levels, to avoid blocking the views. The white walls and wooden floor correspond with the minimalistic character of the exterior and enhance the brightness inside the house. The already spacious living area on the ground floor is extended on the garden side out to a large terrace built on the same level. A short flight of stairs leads to the garden.

Das lange, schmale Grundstück, auf dem die Villa gebaut ist, inspirierte diese etwas außergewöhnliche Kombination aus einem massiven rechteckigen Sockel und voll verglasten Giebelenden, die von einem Satteldach bedeckt sind. Der Kontrast zwischen den dicken Mauern in der Länge und den klaren Öffnungen in der Breite wird durch die Höhe des Gebäudes noch verstärkt, da das Haus drei Stockwerke hoch ist. Das Untergeschoss ist von außen kaum sichtbar. Auf der Gartenseite ist es komplett geschlossen und sieht wie eine Fußleiste aus. Obwohl er zur Hälfte unter der Erde liegt, ist dieser Teil der Villa, zu dem auch eine abgetrennte Wohnung gehört, dank der Fenster an der gegenüberliegenden Fassade nicht dem natürlichen Licht entzogen. Das gesamte Haus ist hell und diskret eingerichtet, um den Eigentümern komfortable und große Innenräume zu bieten. Selbst die Treppe zwischen den Stockwerken hat eine leichte Struktur, die in den oberen Stockwerken halbtransparent wird, um die Aussicht nicht zu versperren. Die weißen Wände und der Holzfußboden passen zum minimalistischen Charakter des Außenraums und verstärken die Helligkeit im Inneren des Hauses. Das bereits sehr geräumige Wohnzimmer im Erdgeschoss wird auf der Gartenseite durch eine große, ebenerdig angelegte Terrasse erweitert. Eine Treppe führt in den Garten.

La parcelle longue et étroite sur laquelle la villa est construite a inspiré cette alliance un peu surprenante d'une base rectangulaire massive recouverte d'un toit en pente avec des extrémités en forme de pignon entièrement vitrées. Le contraste que forment les murs épais dans la longueur avec les ouvertures claires dans la largeur est accentué par la hauteur de la construction puisque la maison compte de trois étages. Le sous-sol est à peine visible de l'extérieur. Côté jardin, il est entièrement fermé et ressemble à une plinthe. Bien qu'à moitié enfouie sous terre, cette partie de la villa qui comprend un appartement individuel n'est cependant pas privée de lumière naturelle grâce aux fenêtres de la façade opposée. Toute la maison est lumineuse et meublée discrètement pour offrir aux propriétaires des intérieurs confortables et spacieux. Même l'escalier entre les étages possède une structure légère qui devient semi-transparente aux étages supérieurs pour éviter de bloquer les vues. Les murs blancs et le plancher en bois correspondent au caractère minimaliste de l'extérieur et renforcent la luminosité à l'intérieur de la maison. La salle de séjour déjà très spacieuse du rez-de-chaussée est prolongée côté jardin par une grande terrasse construite au même niveau. Une volée d'escaliers mène au jardin.

Exterior view

Außenansicht

Vue extérieure

Interiors Innenräume Intérieurs

QUADRANT HOUSE

WARSAW, POLAND

Following a brief to create a simple, sunny, and relaxing home that would react to the movement of the sun during the day, the architects envisioned a highly unique concept. A regular solid volume covered with an untypically shaped gable roof was split into two. The ground floor part with flat roofing runs along the street, while the upper level sits transversely on top of it. This solution provides maximum privacy to the owners and reduces street noise. The highlight of the house is a mechanised terrace inspired by the quadrant, an old device used to determine the position of the stars. Programmed to follow the sun's path, it provides a shadowed and airy outdoor space for relaxing. The drive system is in constant motion during the day to let natural grass grow underneath. Another ingenious solution are the windows in the living room area, which are equipped with an automatic sliding system that makes it possible to open both sides onto the garden. The monolithic character is also the main motif in the interiors, which are dominated by the colour white.

Die Aufgabe der Architekten bestand darin, ein einfaches, sonniges und erholsames Haus zu bauen, das sich der Bewegung der Sonne am Tag anpasst. Sie entwickelten dafür ein einzigartiges Konzept; das rechteckige, zweigeschossige Gebäude, das mit einem ungewöhnlich gestalteten Giebeldach bedeckt ist, wurde horizontal halbiert. Das flach gedeckte Erdgeschoss verläuft entlang der Straße, während das Obergeschoss quer darüber liegt. Diese Lösung bietet den Eigentümern maximale Privatsphäre und reduziert den Straßenlärm. Eine mechanisierte Terrasse, die vom Quadranten inspiriert ist, einem alten Gerät, das in der Astronomie zur Bestimmung der Position der Sterne verwendet wird, vervollständigt dieses einzigartige Ensemble. Die Terrasse, die so programmiert ist, dass sie dem Verlauf der Sonne folgt, bietet einen schattigen und luftigen Außenraum zum Entspannen. Das mechanische System ist tagsüber in ständiger Bewegung, damit darunter Gras wachsen kann. Eine weitere originelle Lösung: Die Wohnzimmerfenster sind mit einem automatischen Schiebesystem ausgestattet, das es ermöglicht, beide Seiten zum Garten hin zu öffnen. Der Minimalismus der Außenbereiche findet sich in den vorwiegend in Weiß gestalteten Innenräumen wieder.

Les architectes avaient pour mission de bâtir une maison simple, ensoleillée et propice au repos qui s'adapterait au mouvement du soleil pendant la journée. Ils ont imaginé pour cela un concept tout à fait unique ; le bâtiment rectangulaire de deux étages, recouvert d'un toit à pignon de forme atypique, a été coupé en deux à l'horizontale. Le rez-de-chaussée à toit plat longe la rue, tandis que l'étage supérieur se trouve posé perpendiculairement au-dessus. Cette solution offre un maximum d'intimité aux propriétaires et réduit le bruit venant de la rue. Une terrasse mécanisée inspirée du quadrant, un ancien appareil utilisé notamment en astronomie pour déterminer la position des étoiles, complète cet ensemble singulier. Programmée pour suivre la course du soleil, la terrasse offre un espace extérieur ombragé et aéré pour se détendre. Le système mécanique est en mouvement constant pendant la journée pour laisser pousser l'herbe en dessous. Autre solution ingénieuse : les fenêtres du salon sont équipées d'un système coulissant automatique qui permet d'ouvrir les deux côtés sur le jardin. Les intérieurs, où le blanc domine, sont conçus dans le même esprit minimaliste que les extérieurs.

ARCHITECTS: ROBERT KONIECZNY – KWK PROMES /// **COMPLETION:** 2018 /// **FURTHER PARTICIPANTS:** KORNEL SZYNDLER (CONSTRUCTION), PULVA ADAM PULWICKI (INTERIOR ARRANGEMENTS) /// **FLOOR AREA:** 558 M² (6,006 FT²) /// **PHOTOS:** JULIUSZ SOKOŁOWSKI

Street façade

Straßenansicht

Façade côté rue

Façade opening up towards the garden and the movement of the terrace

Fassade an der Gartenseite und Bewegung der mechanisierten Terrasse

Façade côté jardin et mouvement de la terrasse

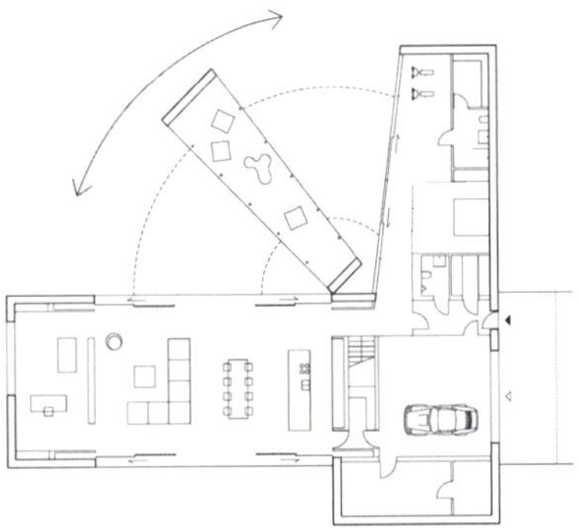

Exterior views Außenansichte Vues extérieure

ARCHITECTS: INDEX ARCHITECTES SARL /// **COMPLETION:** 2016 /// **FLOOR AREA:** 200 M^2 (2,150 FT^2) /// **PHOTOS:** PHILIPPE JONER

THE VILLAGE HOUSE

VILLARLOD, SWITZERLAND

Situated in the middle of a picturesque Swiss village, the house relates to the neighbouring farmhouses and barns. The architects used the archetypical house shape for its timeless character, with numerous possible spatial arrangements. Their work, however, is an interpretation of the tradition with a modern twist. To create a monolithic impression, the roof and one of the façades, as well as the gable sides, are covered with small flat tiles. In contrast, the south-west façade is made of wood, as it is less exposed to both wind and rain thanks to its orientation and protective canopy. Inside the house is a sequence of areas, creating one continuous open space under the large roof. Some of the common spaces like the living room are two floors high, while other rooms are located on two separate levels. The solid volume is enhanced by uniform interiors which are all in white. The numerous flat and extensive monochrome surfaces also contrast interestingly with the rich outer shell.

Mitten in einem malerischen Schweizer Dorf gelegen, ist die Villa im Stil der umliegenden Bauernhöfe und Scheunen gehalten. Die Architekten haben diese archetypische Form des Dorfhauses gewählt, da es zeitlos ist und viele Gestaltungsmöglichkeiten bietet. Die traditionelle Bauform wurde jedoch in eine moderne Formensprache übersetzt. Um den Eindruck eines Monolithen zu erwecken, sind das Dach, eine der Fassaden und beide Giebelseiten mit kleinen, flachen Ziegeln bedeckt. Die südwestliche Fassade ist aus Holz, da sie aufgrund ihrer Ausrichtung und ihres schützenden Vordachs weniger Wind und Regen ausgesetzt ist. Das Innere des Hauses ist eine Abfolge von Räumen, die unter dem großen Dach einen durchgehenden offenen Raum bilden. Einige der Räume, wie das Wohnzimmer, befinden sich auf zwei Etagen, während andere nur auf einer Ebene liegen. Die Wirkung des großzügigen Raumes wird durch das einheitlich in Weiß gehaltene Interieur noch verstärkt. Diese zahlreichen monochromen Flächen bilden einen interessanten Kontrast zum Äußeren des Hauses.

Située au milieu d'un village suisse pittoresque, la villa est dans le style des fermes et des granges avoisinantes. Les architectes ont utilisé cette forme archétypique de maison villageoise pour son caractère intemporel car elle offre de nombreuses possibilités d'aménagement. Leur œuvre est cependant une réinterprétation de la tradition avec une touche de modernité. Pour créer une impression de monolithe, le toit, l'une des façades ainsi que les deux côtés en pignon sont recouverts de petites tuiles plates. La façade sud-ouest est en bois car elle est moins exposée au vent et à la pluie grâce à son orientation et à son auvent de protection. L'intérieur de la maison est une succession de pièces formant un espace ouvert continu sous le grand toit. Certaines des pièces, comme la salle de séjour, s'élèvent sur deux étages, tandis que d'autres ne sont que sur un niveau. Les grands volumes sont mis en valeur par des intérieurs uniformes peints en blanc. Ces nombreuses surfaces monochromes plates contrastent de façon intéressante avec l'enveloppe extérieure de la maison.

Interiors Innenräume Intérieurs

HAUS AM ALBTRAUF

GERMANY

Located in a densely built residential area, the house makes the best of a long and narrow plot. The architect cut out different volumes from the building's structure to let the sun reach deep into the villa, on the one hand, but also to create a sequence of fluidly connected rooms, atriums, and loggias. The generous living area is subtly divided into various zones and lit from two or three sides. The natural light shapes the interiors, which are otherwise designed in a resolutely minimalistic style. Despite the limitations of the plot, the architecture gives the impression of extensive space with dynamically changing perspectives depending on one's location. The impressive west façade with its glazed walls and flat roof resembles a pavilion and opens onto the adjacent garden. The outside–inside relation offers barrier-free access to the natural surroundings of the house from each room. This elegant solution contrasts sharply with the voluminous entrance façade. The latter is closed to provide privacy with the exception of the atrium that illuminates the entrance area. Hidden in the basement are the garage and technical spaces, as well as an office.

Das Haus liegt in einem dicht bebauten Wohngebiet und nutzt ein langes, schmales Grundstück optimal aus. Der Architekt hat Stücke aus der Gebäudestruktur herausgeschnitten, um nicht nur die Sonne überall eindringen zu lassen, sondern auch eine Reihe von Räumen, Atrien und Loggien zu schaffen, die miteinander verbunden sind. Der Wohnbereich ist in verschiedene Bereiche unterteilt und von mehreren Seiten beleuchtet. Natürliches Licht prägt die in einem entschieden minimalistischen Stil gestalteten Innenräume. Trotz der durch das Gelände auferlegten Einschränkungen vermittelt die Architektur den Eindruck eines großen Raumes mit je nach Standort wechselnden Perspektiven. Die beeindruckende Westfassade mit ihren Glaswänden und dem Flachdach ähnelt einem Pavillon und öffnet sich zum angrenzenden Garten. Die Beziehung zwischen außen und innen wird von dem Anliegen dominiert, von jedem Raum aus einen leichten Übergang vom Haus in die natürliche Umgebung zu ermöglichen. Dieser elegante und fließende Grundriss steht in scharfem Kontrast zu der massiveren Eingangsfassade. Letztere ist vollständig geschlossen, um eine gewisse Intimität zu gewährleisten, mit Ausnahme des Atriums, das den Eingang beleuchtet. Im Untergeschoss befinden sich die Garage und die Technikräume.

Située dans un quartier résidentiel densément bâti, la maison tire le meilleur parti d'un terrain long et étroit. L'architecte a taillé dans les volumes de la structure du bâtiment non seulement pour que le soleil y pénètre partout, mais aussi pour créer une suite de pièces, d'atriums et de loggias reliées l'une à l'autre. Le vaste séjour est subtilement divisé en différentes zones et éclairé de plusieurs côtés. La lumière naturelle façonne les intérieurs conçus dans un style résolument minimaliste. Malgré les limites imposées par le terrain, l'architecture donne l'impression d'un espace étendu avec des perspectives qui changent en fonction de l'endroit où l'on se trouve. L'impressionnante façade ouest, avec ses murs vitrés et son toit plat, ressemble à un pavillon et s'ouvre sur le jardin adjacent. La relation extérieur-intérieur est dominée par le souci d'offrir un passage aisé de la maison à l'environnement naturel depuis chaque pièce. Cet aménagement élégant et fluide contraste fortement avec la façade d'entrée plus massive. Cette dernière est entièrement cloisonnée pour garantir une certaine intimité, à l'exception de l'atrium qui éclaire l'entrée. Le garage et les locaux techniques, ainsi qu'un bureau, sont cachés au sous-sol.

Street façade

Fassade an der Straßenseite

Façade côté rue

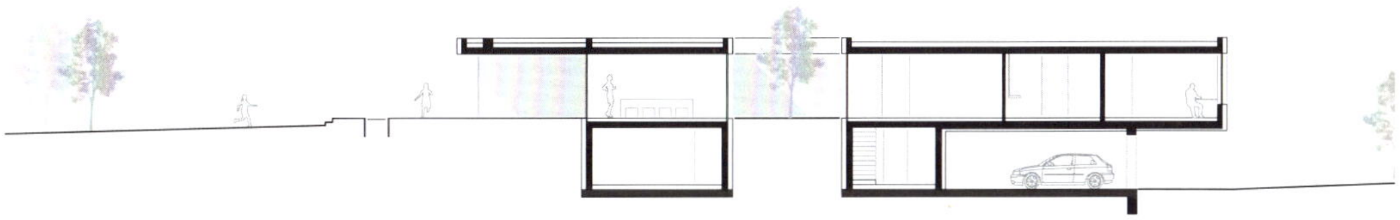

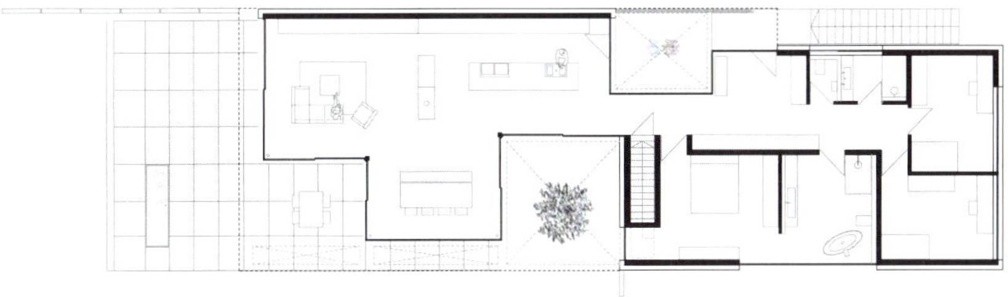

Terrace view

Blick auf die Terrasse

Vue sur la terrasse

Section Schnitt Section

Main floor plan

Gesamtübersicht

Plan d'ensemble

ARCHITECTS: LIEBEL/ARCHITEKTEN BDA /// **COMPLETION:** 2018 /// **FLOOR AREA:** 251 M² (2,701 FT²) /// **PHOTOS:** BRIGIDA GONZÁLEZ

Exterior view Außenansicht Vue extérieure

Interiors Innenräume Intérieurs

Patio

VILLA BAKKUM

CASTRICUM, THE NETHERLANDS

Sitting at the edge of Kennemerland National Park, the house was designed to blend into the landscape. The tripod-shaped two-storey structure is divided into living and working areas, each of which occupies an individual wing. They are connected by a triangular central hall. The three main volumes of the house are covered with gabled roofs that slope steeply, influencing the top floor interiors, which look more like attic rooms. The architects also used the roof to merge the volume with the context and give it a distinctive character. The private part with an inner corner opens onto the garden. The kitchen and living room, already very spacious, have access to additional space outside. Large windows on both levels as well as the wood finish on this elevation soften the transition between the architecture and surrounding nature. The other façades are contrastingly made of particularly layered brick, which creates a visually curious horizontal relief. The inventive shape as well as this rich texture of the outer shell create a play of light. The house therefore looks quite different from various angles and throughout a day.

Das am Rande des Kennemerland Nationalparks gelegene Haus wurde so geplant, dass es sich in die Landschaft einfügt. Seine zweigeschossige, dreiflügelige Struktur ist in Wohn- und Arbeitsbereiche unterteilt, die jeweils einen separaten Flügel belegen. Der Wohnraum ist durch eine zentrale dreieckige Halle mit den Arbeitsräumen verbunden. Die drei Flügel, aus denen das Haus besteht, sind mit steil abfallenden Satteldächern bedeckt, die die Innenaufteilung des ersten Stockwerks beeinflussen; seine Struktur erinnert an eine Abfolge von Mansardenzimmern. Die Architekten nutzten auch die verschiedenen Teile des Daches, um jedem der Flügel des Hauses einen unverwechselbaren Charakter zu geben, was auch dazu beiträgt, dass es sich in die Landschaft einfügt. So bildet der Wohnraum einen Winkel, der sich zum Garten hin öffnet. Die geräumige Küche und das Wohnzimmer gewinnen dadurch ein wenig zusätzlichen Platz im Freien. Große Fenster entlang der Fassade und ihre Holzausführung verwischen den Übergang zwischen dem Gebäude und der umgebenden Natur. Die beiden anderen Fassaden bestehen aus laminiertem Ziegelstein, wodurch ein optisch interessantes horizontales Relief entsteht. Die einzigartige Form der Villa und die reichhaltige Textur der Außenhülle fördern das Lichtspiel. Das Haus sieht daher je nach dem gewählten Blickwinkel und der Tageszeit sehr unterschiedlich aus.

Située en bordure du parc national de Kennemerland, la maison a été conçue pour se fondre dans le paysage. Sa structure en forme de trépied à deux étages est divisée en zones d'habitation et de travail ; chacune d'elles occupe une aile séparée. L'espace d'habitation est relié aux pièces à usage professionnel par un hall central triangulaire. Les trois ailes qui composent la maison sont recouvertes de toits à pignon dont les pentes sont très prononcées ce qui influence d'ailleurs l'aménagement intérieur du premier étage ; son aspect fait penser à une succession de pièces mansardées. Les architectes ont également utilisé les différentes parties du toit pour donner à chacune des ailes de la maison un trait distinctif qui l'aide aussi à s'inscrire dans le paysage. Ainsi, l'espace d'habitation forme un angle qui s'ouvre sur le jardin. La cuisine et le salon, très spacieux, y gagnent encore un peu d'espace supplémentaire à l'extérieur. Les grandes fenêtres sur toute cette façade et sa finition en bois adoucissent la transition entre le bâtiment et la nature environnante. Les deux autres façades sont en briques stratifiées ce qui crée un relief horizontal visuellement intriguant. La forme originale de la villa ainsi que la riche texture de l'enveloppe extérieure favorisent les jeux de lumière. La maison a donc un aspect très différent selon l'angle de vue qu'on choisit et l'heure de la journée.

ARCHITECTS: MOKE ARCHITECTEN GIANNI CITO /// **COMPLETION:** 2017 /// **FURTHER PARTICIPANT:** PATRICK DE WEERD (PROJECT LEADER), ENGINEERING BREED (INTEGRATED DESIGN) /// **FLOOR AREA:** 400 M² (4,305 FT²) /// **PHOTOS:** THIJS WOLZAK

Exterior view Außenansicht Vue extérieure

Interiors Innenräume Intérieurs

Terrace view

Blick auf die Terrasse

Vue sur la terrasse

HHCR – HOUSEHUT CORTICELLA

CORTICELLA, ITALY

This spectacular Dalmatian-like black and white villa is built into the horizon line on the bank of the Tresinaro River. The architects designed it as a reinterpretation of a historical countryside house using an inventive take on typical forms. The horizontal composition of volumes, visually anchoring the house to the plot despite its significant size, is made of two parallel wings linked by an impressive double-height living space, as well as through a suspended balcony. This space is the heart of the structure and, thanks to huge windows, forms a transparent connection with the outside. The ground floor has an open-space plan, which in combination with its numerous geometric openings creates a grandiose interior, encompassing the kitchen and dining area. Additionally, the porch, framed structurally with a jasmine canopy, forms an open-air extension of the living space with a pool in the garden. To enhance the geometry with light, the architects not only found original locations for the windows across both levels but also visually emphasised them with special carvings and the use of black against walls that are otherwise white. The colour white also dominates the interiors with the exception of the wooden floors.

Diese spektakuläre, Dalmatiner-ähnliche, schwarz-weiß gesprenkelte Villa ist auf einer Horizontlinie am Ufer des Flusses Tresinaro gebaut. Die Architekten interpretierten den traditionellen Bautyp des Landhauses neu und übersetzen seine Struktur in eine eigene Formensprache. Horizontale Bauelemente tragen dazu bei, dass das Haus trotz seiner Größe im Grundstück verankert ist. Eine der Besonderheiten der Villa ist ihre Struktur, die durch die beiden parallelen, sich in entgegengesetzte Richtungen erstreckenden Flügel gekennzeichnet ist. Sie sind durch einen beeindruckenden zweigeschossigen Wohnraum und einen abgehängten Balkon verbunden. Der zentrale Wohnraum ist das Herzstück des Gebäudes. Dank seiner großen Fenster besitzt es einen quasi unsichtbaren Übergang nach außen. Das Erdgeschoss besticht durch seinen offenen Grundriss, der im Zusammenspiel mit geometrischen Öffnungen einen großen und eindrucksvollen Innenraum bildet, der Küche und Esszimmer umfasst. Darüber hinaus bildet die von einem Jasmin-Baldachin eingerahmte Veranda eine Erweiterung des Wohnzimmers im Freien mit einem Pool im Garten. Die Fenster sind nicht nur so platziert, dass sie die geometrischen Formen des Hauses betonen, sondern auch die Wirkung des Lichteinfalls verstärken. Ausserdem sind sie mit Schnitzereien und schwarzen Rändern umrahmt, die stark mit den weißen Wänden kontrastieren. Auch in den Interieurs ist Weiß vorherrschend, mit Ausnahme der Holzböden.

Cette spectaculaire villa tachetée de noir et blanc, à l'instar des dalmatiens, est construite sur une ligne d'horizon au bord du fleuve Tresinaro. Les architectes l'ont conçue comme une réinterprétation d'une maison de campagne classique dont les formes traditionnelles auraient été audacieusement retravaillées. Malgré leurs dimensions importantes, les corps de bâtiment, grâce à leur horizontalité, s'ancrent dans le terrain. L'une des singularités de la villa est sa structure marquée par les deux ailes parallèles qui se déploient dans des directions opposées. Elles sont reliées par une imposante salle de séjour sur deux étages ainsi que par un balcon suspendu. L'espace de séjour est au cœur de la structure. Grâce à ses fenêtres gigantesques, il offre une transition lumineuse avec l'extérieur. Le rez-de-chaussée forme une pièce unique jalonnée d'ouvertures géométriques qui le transforment en un vaste intérieur englobant la cuisine et la salle à manger. Par ailleurs, le porche, encadré par un auvent de jasmin, crée une extension en plein air du séjour avec une piscine dans le jardin. Pour rendre hommage aux formes géométriques et à la lumière, les architectes ont non seulement placé les fenêtres de façon insolite sur les deux étages, mais ils les ont également mis en valeur avec des découpes spéciales et des bordures noires qui contrastent avec les murs blancs. Le blanc est la couleur dominante à l'intérieur à l'exception des parquets en bois.

Swimming pool and open porch

Swimmingpool und offene Veranda

Piscine et portique ouvert

Terrace view

Blick auf die Terrasse

Vue sur la terrasse

Exterior view Außenansicht Vue extérieure

ARCHITECTS: NAT OFFICE - CHRISTIAN GASPARINI ARCHITECT /// **COMPLETION:** 2018 /// **FURTHER PARTICIPANTS:** LUIGI SALVO (STRUCTURES), BARBARA PONTI (LANDSCAPE DESIGN), SUSANNA MAZZONI UPO (LIGHTING DESIGN) /// **FLOOR AREA:** 350 M² (3,767 FT²) /// **PHOTOS:** FILIPPO POLI

Open-space living and dining area

Offenes Wohn- und Esszimmer

Salon et salle à manger en espace ouvert

Staircase Escalier Treppe

Interior on the first floor

Innenraum (Obergeschoss)

Intérieur (premier étage)

Section Schnitt Section

Exterior view Außenansicht Vue extérieure

MAMI HOUSE

MATOSINHOS, PORTO, PORTUGAL

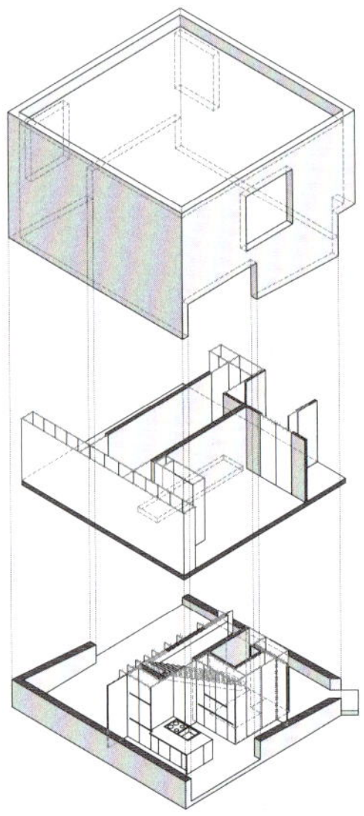

The two-storey MAMI house occupies the flat ground towards the west of the plot, which is shaped like pizza-slice with a corner. The purity of the cubic structure of the house is visually striking. The façades balance between the pure solid walls and the few yet large windows placed irregularly on both floors. To meet the owners' low budget brief, the architects started by revising the potentially most expensive components of the house and limited the number of bathrooms to one per level. Materials were also selected mainly for their energy-efficient qualities rather than for an expensive finishing look. The architects envisioned a mini-bunker made of reinforced concrete, the spatial arrangement of which is characterised by a similar minimalistic approach. In the middle of the ground floor, a wooden block, a cube in a cube, contains the kitchen, the toilet, the stairs, and the living room shelves. Thanks to this solution, playing with geometry, the space of the lower level is effectively divided without using wall partitions. The upstairs space is more private and encompasses three bedrooms and a toilette. The minimalistic interiors are modern with the pure combination of exposed concrete, warm wood, and white furnishings.

Diese zweigeschossige Villa befindet sich auf einem flachen Grundstück, deren Form einem Pizzastück ähnelt. Seine kubische Struktur mit sehr reinen Linien fällt ins Auge. Die Fassaden weisen Kontraste zwischen massiven, einteiligen Wänden und großen, unregelmäßig angeordneten Fenstern auf. Um das von den Eigentümern festgelegte begrenzte Budget einzuhalten, reduzierten die Architekten die teuersten Teile des Gebäudes. Insbesondere beschränkten sie die Anzahl der Badezimmer auf ein Badezimmer pro Stockwerk. Die Materialien wurden eher nach ihren Energieeffizienzqualitäten als nach ihrem Veredelungsgrad ausgewählt. Die Architekten entwarfen einen Stahlbeton-Minibunker, dessen Innenausstattung sich ebenfalls durch seinen minimalistischen Ansatz auszeichnet. Im Erdgeschoss bildet ein großer Holzblock in der Mitte des Raumes einen Kubus. In diesem Block befinden sich die Küche, die Toilette, das Treppenhaus und die Regale des Wohnraums. Dank dieser originellen Baulösung kommt das untere Stockwerk ohne Trennwände aus. Der erste Stock, der für den privaten Gebrauch bestimmt ist, umfasst drei Schlafzimmer und ein Badezimmer. Die minimalistischen Innenräume sind durch eine moderne und raffinierte Kombination aus Sichtbeton, Warmtonholz und weißen Möbeln geprägt.

Cette villa à deux étages occupe un terrain plat à l'ouest d'une parcelle dont la forme ressemble à celle d'un morceau de pizza. Sa structure cubique aux lignes très épurées attire le regard. Les façades offrent toutes un contraste entre des murs massifs d'un seul tenant et de grandes fenêtres disposées assez irrégulièrement. Pour respecter le budget limité fixé par les propriétaires, les architectes ont revu à la baisse les parties les plus coûteuses de la construction. Ils ont notamment limité le nombre de salles de bain à une par étage. Les matériaux ont été sélectionnés pour leur efficacité énergétique plutôt que pour leur aspect de finition. Les architectes ont conçu un mini-bunker en béton armé dont l'agencement intérieur se caractérise aussi par son approche minimaliste. Au rez-de-chaussée, un grand bloc en bois disposé au milieu de l'espace forme un cube. Ce bloc accueille la cuisine, les toilettes, l'escalier et les étagères du salon. Grâce à cette solution qui joue avec la géométrie, l'étage inférieur est ingénieusement divisé sans qu'on ait recours à des cloisons. Le premier étage, réservé à un usage privé, comprend trois chambres et une salle de toilette. Les intérieurs minimalistes sont marqués par une alliance moderne et épurée de béton apparent, de bois aux teintes chaudes et de mobilier blanc.

ARCHITECTS: NOARQ - JOSÉ CARLOS NUNES DE OLIVEIRA /// **COMPLETION:** 2016 /// **FURTHER PARTICIPANTS:** GONÇALO FERREIRA, HUGO ARAUJO (ARCHITECTS), AFONSO SERRA NEVES (STRUCTURAL PROJECT), ROSSANA PEREIRA (HYDRAULIC AND ACUSTIC PROJECT), ALEXANDRE MARTINS (ELECTRICITY, TELECOMMUNICATIONS AND SECURITY), RAUL BESSA (GAS AND HVAC PROJECT), PEDRO SOUSA-SOCIEDADE UNIPESSOAL, LDA; ORDEP MOBILIÁRIO (CONSTRUCTORS) /// **FLOOR AREA:** 162 M^2 (1,744 FT^2) /// **PHOTOS:** JOÃO MORGADO

Interiors Innenräume Intérieurs

ARCHITECTS: NICOLA PROBST ARCHITETTI /// **COMPLETION:** 2019 /// **FLOOR AREA:** 1,170 M² (12,595 FT²) ///
PHOTOS: ALEXANDRE ZVEIGER

Exterior view Außenansicht Vue extérieure

Terrace Terrasse Terrasse

VILLA 4L_

LUGANO, SWITZERLAND

This multilevel urban villa is divided into three apartments, one large space dynamically embracing two smaller flats. The architects incorporated the structure into the steep hill using large inclined pillars that support the retaining walls. They are central to the project, mainly as elements indicating the internal and external spaces. The inventive lighting system creates a spectacular sculptural effect when it's dark. Villa 4L_ is an intriguing compilation of volumes and voids, with a system of terraces and glazed walls enveloping numerous spaces from various sides to offer panoramic vistas. They all significantly extend the interiors and open them, particularly on the higher levels, to the mountainous landscape. The main apartment has three floors. A spacious living room at its heart has been planned as a void surrounded by a swimming pool, a terrace, a mineral garden, and service area. The villa, extremely dynamic and light at the same, offers an extensive and bright space for everyday life with a flair. The architects also planned several eco solutions, like a heat pump, and photo voltaic and thermal solar panels that guarantee energy sustainability.

Diese städtische, mehrstöckige Villa ist in drei Wohnungen unterteilt, von denen eine große zwei kleinere Wohnungen dynamisch umfasst. Die Architekten haben das Gebäude in dem steilen Gelände mithilfe von großen, schräg stehenden Pfeilern verankert, die die Stützmauern stabilisieren. Sie sind ein zentrales Element des Projektes, weil sie die Grenze zwischen den Innen- und Außenbereichen markieren. Ein ausgeklügeltes Beleuchtungssystem erzeugt bei Nacht ein eindrucksvolles Spiel der Formen. Die Villa 4L_ ist eine faszinierende Sammlung voller und leerer Räume mit Terrassen und Glaswänden, die die Außenflächen bedecken und so einen Panoramablick bieten. Sie erweitern so die Innenräume und öffnen sie, vor allem in den oberen Stockwerken, zur Berglandschaft. Die Hauptwohnung hat drei Stockwerke. Ein geräumiges Wohnzimmer in seiner Mitte ist als leerer Raum gedacht, der von einem Schwimmbad, einer Terrasse, einem Mineraliengarten und einem Servicebereich umgeben ist. Die gleichzeitig markante als auch leicht wirkende Villa bietet einen hellen, komfortablen Lebensraum mit behaglichem Ambiente. Die Architekten haben auch mehrere ökologische Lösungen wie eine Wärmepumpe, Photovoltaik- und thermische Solarkollektoren entwickelt, die die energetische Nachhaltigkeit des Hauses garantieren.

Cette villa urbaine à plusieurs étages est divisée en trois appartements, dont un grand qui englobe de façon dynamique deux appartements plus petits. Les architectes ont arrimé la structure à la colline escarpée avec des grands piliers inclinés qui supportent des murs de soutènement. Ces piliers sont au cœur du projet architectural car ils délimitent l'intérieur et l'extérieur. Un système d'éclairage ingénieux crée un jeu de sculptures surprenant lorsqu'il fait nuit. La Villa 4L_ est un ensemble fascinant d'espaces pleins et vides doté de terrasses et de murs vitrés qui recouvrent les surfaces extérieures pour offrir des vues panoramiques. Ils prolongent ainsi les intérieurs et les ouvrent sur le paysage montagneux, notamment aux étages supérieurs. L'appartement principal compte trois étages. Un salon spacieux en son centre se présente comme un espace vide entouré d'une piscine, d'une terrasse, d'un jardin minéral et d'une zone de service. Vivante et lumineuse, la villa forme un vaste espace clair pour la vie quotidienne agrémenté d'une touche de sophistication. Les architectes ont également imaginé plusieurs solutions écologiques comme une pompe à chaleur, des panneaux solaires photovoltaïques et thermiques qui garantissent la durabilité énergétique de la maison.

Terrace view

Blick auf die Terrasse

Vue sur la terrasse

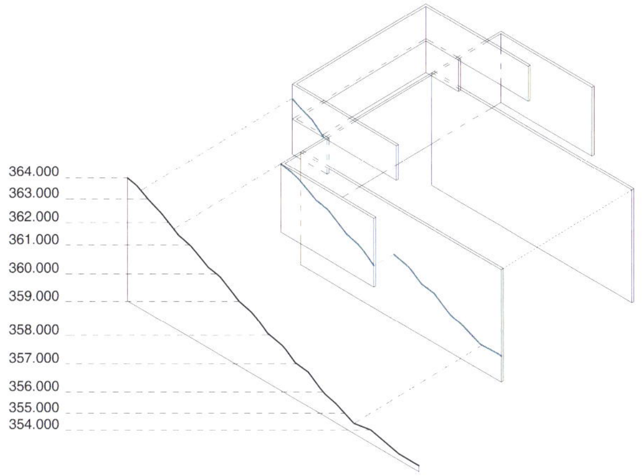

Wall structure Wandstruktur Structure des murs

Interiors Innenräume Intérieurs

Staircase Escalier Treppe

ARCHITECTS: NOARQ - JOSÉ CARLOS NUNES DE OLIVEIRA /// **COMPLETION:** 2018 /// **FURTHER PARTICIPANTS:** HUGO ARAÚJO, ANDRÉ OLIVEIRA, JOANA LEITE PINTO, LUÍS LIMA, DANIEL VIANA, JULIANA COSTA (ARCHITECTS), FRANCISCO BERNARDO, DIOGO DRUMOND (STRUCTURES), TÂNIA MATOS (HYDRAULICS), ALEXANDRE MARTINS (ELECTRICITY, TELECOMMUNICATIONS AND SECURITY), EDIGREEN – RUI LIMA, GONÇALO LEAL (GAS AND CLIMATIZATION), CONCEITO RECENTE; BBG - HYLINE; TOPMARMI, LDA.; ORDEP MOBILIÁRIO; TOPGREEN; O BIBELOT; GONÇALO SERRA LOBO SERRALHARIA UNIPESSOAL; NUNO MIRANDA INSTALAÇÕES AVAC, UNIPESSOAL LDA (CONSTRUCTORS) /// **FLOOR AREA:** 643 M^2 (6,921 FT^2) /// **PHOTOS:** FERNANDO GUERRA

RPFV HOUSE

SANTO TIRSO, PORTO, PORTUGAL

The plot is part of a steep west-east slope divided into two terraces. In a gigantic area of 1697 square meters (18,266 ft^2) only 600 square meters (6,458 ft^2) were available to build on, as the rest is part of an Agricultural Reserve. As a result, the structure of the house is moved far from the street and surrounded by the restricted land. The three-storey construction of super-imposed volumes is based on a former residential building. On the ground floor, the new and old architecture coexist, housing social functions and a patio. The original structure used to be a cellar and now supports ventilation and is a source of light for the interiors. One level higher, a larger patio organises the first floor, where spaces are used as the family's everyday living area. The more private second floor, used for relaxation, includes three bedrooms. The architects' goal was to create a structure that would be in a dialogue with the context as it merges into the topography, as well as to respect the memory of the original house.

Das Grundstück, auf dem die Villa gebaut wurde, liegt an einem steilen West-Ost-Hang und ist in zwei Terrassen unterteilt. Seine Gesamtfläche beträgt 1.697 m^2, aber nur 600 m^2 Land konnten bebaut werden, da der Rest Teil eines landwirtschaftlichen Reservats ist. Daher wurde das Haus weit von der Straße entfernt auf dem einzigen genehmigten Grundstück gebaut. Das dreigeschossige Gebäude mit übereinanderliegenden Baukörpern nimmt teilweise Elemente eines älteren Wohnhauses auf. Im Erdgeschoss bestehen Alt und Neu harmonisch nebeneinander und beherbergen die Empfangsräume und einen Innenhof. Letzterer, der früher ein Keller war, dient heute als Lichtquelle für die Innenräume und sorgt gleichzeitig für natürliche Belüftung. Eine Etage höher strukturiert ein weiterer, geräumigerer Innenhof den ersten Stock mit den Wohnräumen der Familie. Die zweite und letzte Etage verfügt über drei Schlafzimmer. Das Ziel der Architekten war es, ein Gebäude zu erschaffen, das im Dialog mit der topografischen Umgebung steht und die Erinnerung an das ursprüngliche Haus bewahrt.

La parcelle sur laquelle la villa est bâtie se situe sur une pente raide orientée ouest-est. Cette parcelle est scindée en deux terrasses. La surface totale de la parcelle atteint les 1 697 m^2, mais seuls 600 m^2 de terrain étaient constructibles, car le reste fait partie d'une réserve agricole. En conséquence, la maison a été édifiée assez loin de la rue sur la seule parcelle autorisée. La construction de trois étages aux volumes superposés les uns sur les autres reprend en partie des éléments d'une résidence plus ancienne. Au rez-de-chaussée, l'ancien et le nouveau coexistent harmonieusement. Cet étage accueille les pièces de réception et un patio. Ce patio, qui était autrefois une cave, sert aujourd'hui de source de lumière pour les intérieurs tout en assurant leur ventilation naturelle. Un étage plus haut, un autre patio plus spacieux structure le premier étage où les pièces sont utilisées pour la vie quotidienne de la famille. Le deuxième et dernier étage, qui est le plus privé, comprend trois chambres à coucher. L'objectif des architectes était de créer une structure qui serait en dialogue avec l'environnement topographique ainsi que de garder la mémoire de la maison d'origine.

Exterior view Außenansicht Vue extérieure

Sketche Skizze Esquisse

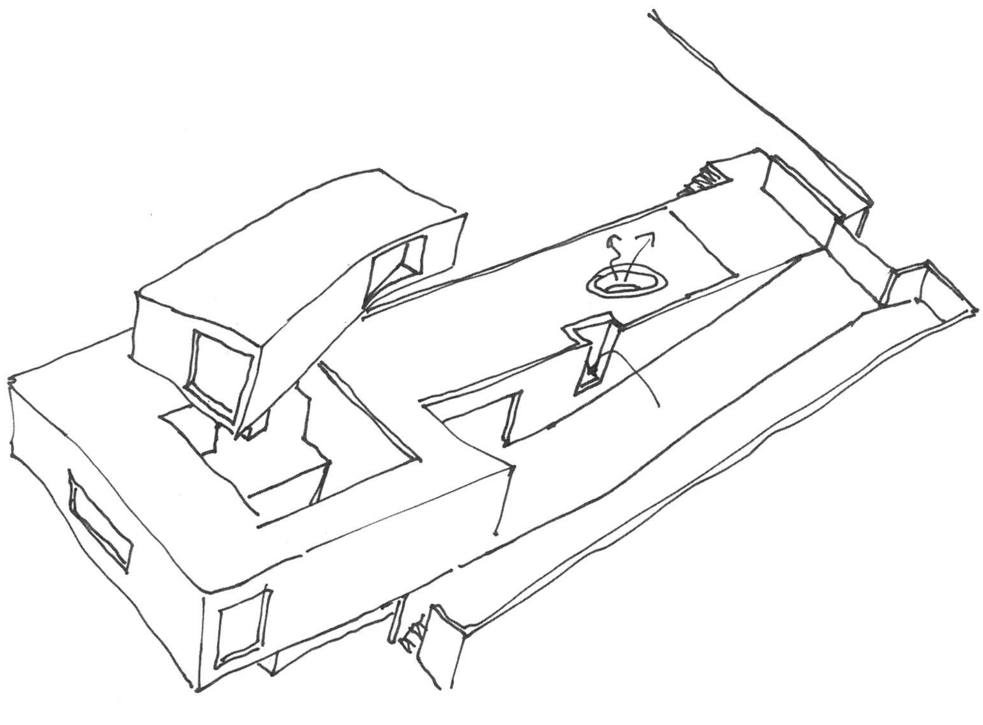

Exterior view *Außenansicht* Vue extérieure

WOHNHAUS FAMILIE BINDER

TEGERFELDEN, SWITZERLAND

This pavilion-like residence is defined by its copper roof, resting on four pairs of supports, which do not however interrupt the continuous glass façade. The architects employed some interesting contrasts: between the traditional shape and very modern materials, and between the light glass base and the massive top. The roof actually looks as if it were floating over the ground. The effect is very interesting – while the structure echoes the historical architecture of the village, the original take on transparent façades is quite a surprise. Particularly surprising is the fact that the building is buried into the terrain and so the bottom part remains slightly hidden behind a slope side. The interior is dominated by timber construction, with deliberately shown joints of the components. The centrally located volume zones the spaces, so there is no need for partitions. The space can be optically separated, however, with sliding doors. The glazed façades create a sense of unrestricted space and open the inside entirely onto the park-like garden with a pool and other smaller buildings. They are all a very original interpretation of the historical context.

Dieses Wohnhaus im Pavillon-Stil wird von seinem imposanten Kupferdach geprägt. Das Dach ruht auf 4 Stützenpaaren, die die durchlaufende Glasfassade nicht unterbrechen. Das Gebäude spiegelt somit zwei von den Architekten beabsichtigte Kontraste wider: einerseits zwischen der traditionellen Form und den sehr modernen Materialien und andererseits zwischen der Leichtigkeit der Glaskonstruktion und dem massiven Charakter des Daches, das manchmal den Eindruck erweckt, über dem Boden zu schweben. Der Effekt ist faszinierend: Während das Dach und die Gesamtsilhouette der Villa die traditionelle Architektur des Dorfes widerspiegeln, ist das ungewöhnliche Erscheinungsbild der transparenten Fassaden recht überraschend. Wie um einen Hauch von Erstaunen hinzuzufügen, ist das Gebäude teilweise im Boden vergraben, sodass die Villa auf einer Seite des Hangs leicht verborgen bleibt. Das Innere der Villa ist mit einer Holzverkleidung verziert, deren Fugen bewusst freigelegt sind. Die Räume sind um einen zentralen Raum herum verteilt, ohne dass Trennwände erforderlich sind. Durch Schiebetüren ist es jedoch möglich, jeden Teil abzugrenzen. Die Glasfassaden vermitteln den Eindruck eines freien Raumes und öffnen den gesamten Innenraum zum Park mit seinem Schwimmbad und anderen kleineren Gebäuden. Sie alle stellen eine sehr originelle Interpretation des traditionellen lokalen Stils dar.

Cette résidence en forme de pavillon d'exposition est dominée par son imposant toit en cuivre. Celui-ci repose sur quatre paires de piliers posés de façon à ne pas obstruer la façade vitrée continue. Le bâtiment reflète ainsi deux contrastes voulus par les architectes : celui, d'une part, entre la forme traditionnelle et les matériaux très modernes et, d'autre part, celui entre la légèreté de la structure en verre et le caractère massif du toit Ce dernier donne parfois l'impression de léviter au-dessus du sol. L'effet obtenu est fascinant : si le toit et la silhouette générale de la villa font écho à l'architecture traditionnelle du village, l'aspect insolite des façades transparentes est assez déroutant. Comme pour rajouter une touche d'étrangeté, le bâtiment est en partie enterré dans le terrain ; la villa se trouve donc légèrement dissimulée d'un côté de la pente. L'intérieur de la villa est décoré d'un revêtement en bois dont les jointures sont délibérément mises à nu. Les pièces sont réparties autour d'un espace central sans qu'il y ait besoin de cloisons. Des portes coulissantes permettent cependant de délimiter chaque partie. Les façades vitrées donnent une impression d'espace libre et ouvrent entièrement l'intérieur sur le parc agrémenté d'une piscine et d'autres bâtiments plus petits. Ils constituent tous une interprétation très originale du style local traditionnel.

ARCHITECTS: OLIVER CHRISTEN ARCHITEKTEN /// **COMPLETION:** 2017 /// **FLOOR AREA:** 123 M² (1,324 FT²) /// **PHOTOS:** OLIVER CHRISTEN ARCHITEKTEN, VALENTIN JECK, STÄFA

Exterior view Außenansicht Vue extérieure

Ground floor plan

Grundriss Erdgeschosses

Plan du rez-de-chaussée

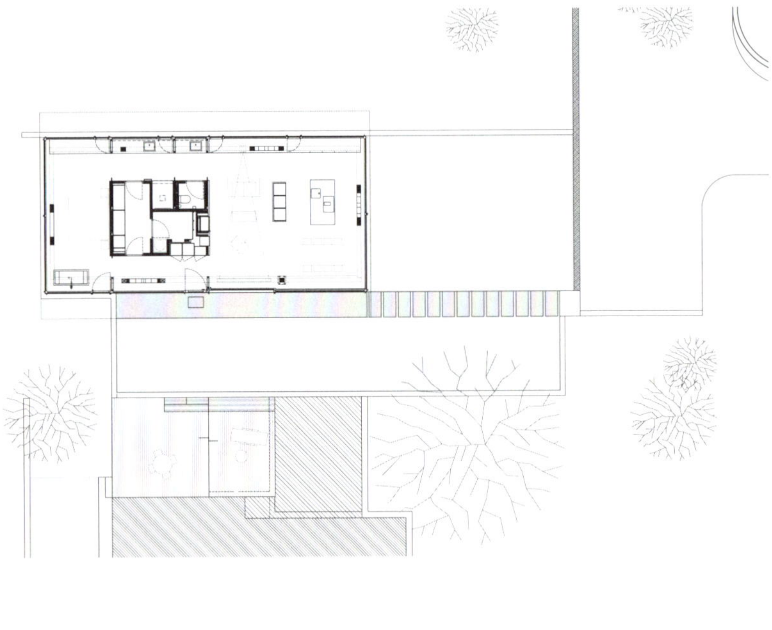

Interiors Innenräume Intérieurs

VILLA SCHATZL-MAYR

PASSAU, GERMANY

The sophisticated and ephemeral volume of Villa Schatzlmayr sits on its extensive plot as if an actor on a stage. Developed horizontally, it overlooks an unobstructed view of flat meadows and the Danube River. The architects fulfilled the owners' dream to have a spacious and one-level residence that would interact with its natural surroundings throughout the year. Constructed of three volumes, the house is practically closed from the street side to provide privacy, and is entirely open on the opposite side to invite the landscape into its elegant interiors. The floor-to-ceiling glazed façade links the vast outdoors to the living area with an open kitchen, dining room, and adjoining fireplace room. The private rooms are also filled with natural light. One interesting element is the long infinity pool, which extends partly into the building and merges visually with the horizon. The two-storey cube at one of the corners is the owners' creative area; it houses two guest apartments. The main entrance to the villa is located between the residential horizontal part and the higher studio. The natural scenery can also be admired on the terrace, which stretches along the entire length of the building.

Die eleganten und diskreten Umrisse der Villa Schatzmayr erheben sich über das weitläufige Grundstück wie ein Schauspieler, der auf einer Bühne wandelt. Ihre horizontale Struktur bietet eine außergewöhnliche Aussicht auf die umliegenden flachen Wiesen und die Ufer der Donau. Die Architekten haben den Traum der Eigentümer erfüllt, ein geräumiges, einstöckiges Wohnhaus zu haben, das das ganze Jahr über mit der Natur interagiert. Das in drei Teilen gebaute Haus ist zur Straßenseite hin fast geschlossen und auf der gegenüberliegenden Seite völlig offen, als ob es die Landschaft in die eleganten Innenräume bringen wollte. Die raumhohe Glasfassade verbindet die Natur mit dem Wohnbereich: Küche, Esszimmer und Kaminzimmer. Auch die Schlafzimmer sind in natürliches Licht getaucht. Das lange Infinity-Swimmingpool, das sich teilweise bis zum Herzen des Gebäudes erstreckt und sich in den Horizont einfügt, ist eine der Besonderheiten der Villa. Der zweigeschossige Kubus an einem Ende des Gebäudes ist der kreative Bereich der Eigentümer. Es beherbergt auch zwei Gästewohnungen. Der Haupteingang der Villa befindet sich zwischen dem Wohnteil und dem oberen Atelier. Die Naturlandschaft kann auch auf der Terrasse bewundert werden, die sich über die gesamte Länge des Gebäudes erstreckt.

La silhouette élégante et discrète de la Villa Schatzmayr se dresse sur toute l'étendue de la parcelle comme un acteur déambulant sur une scène. Sa structure horizontale offre une vue exceptionnelle sur les prairies plates qui l'entourent et sur les rives du Danube. Les architectes ont exaucé le rêve des propriétaires d'avoir une résidence spacieuse et de plain-pied qui interagirait avec la nature tout au long de l'année. Construite en trois parties, la maison est quasiment fermée côté rue pour plus d'intimité et entièrement ouverte à l'opposé comme pour faire entrer le paysage dans les intérieurs élégants. La façade vitrée du sol au plafond relie la nature aux pièces communes : cuisine, salle à manger et salon doté d'une cheminée. Les chambres sont également baignées de lumière naturelle. La longue piscine à débordement qui s'étend en partie au cœur du bâtiment et se fond avec l'horizon est l'une des particularités de la villa. Le cube de deux étages, situé à l'une des extrémités de l'édifice est l'espace de création des propriétaires. Il abrite aussi deux appartements d'hôtes. L'entrée principale de la villa est située entre la partie résidentielle et le studio supérieur. On peut également admirer le paysage naturel sur la terrasse qui s'étend sur toute la longueur du bâtiment.

Street view

Straßenansicht

Façade côté rue

next page
Façade opening up towards the garden

Fassade an der Gartenseite

Façade côté jardin

ARCHITECTS: PHILIPPARCHITEKTEN ANNA PHILIPP /// **COMPLETION:** 2018 /// **FLOOR AREA:** 760 M² (8,180 FT²) ///
PHOTOS: PHILIPPARCHITEKTEN

Pool Swimmingpool Piscine

Street façade

Fassade an der Straßenseite

Façade côté rue

VILLA NEO

ROSENGARTEN, GERMANY

Made of exposed concrete, from the entrance Villa NEO presents itself as a solid and compact intersection of cubic volumes. On the other side, facing the forest, the villa takes on surprising and sculptural forms that play originally with the plot's topography and open the structure to views of the densely wooded landscape. Quintessentially contemporary, the residence pushes boundaries and challenges the traditional idea of a villa. A distinctive statement in its natural context, the building is made of materials determining its characteristic modern look – other than concrete, glass and steel were also used. The inventive L-shape shape offers ample space for flexible arrangements inside. The generous double-height living area on the ground floor contrasts with the upper level which offers inviting and cosy private rooms, thanks to the twisted body of the structure. Large steel lamellas span the structure in the central part to connect both levels. All areas on both storeys are flooded with daylight through the floor-to-ceiling windows. As connections to the outside, these glazed elements also create a visually stark contrast with the otherwise solid materials.

An der Straßenseite zeigt sich die im rohen Beton gebaute Villa NEO als solide und kompakte Kreuzung aus kubischen Modulen. Auf der Waldseite weist die Villa hingegen eine völlig andere Struktur auf: skulpturale Linien, die die topografischen Gegebenheiten widerspiegeln und den Blick auf die bewaldete Landschaft freigeben. Die Residenz ist vollkommen zeitgenössisch. Sie stößt an die Grenzen des Genres und stellt das traditionelle Konzept der Villa in Frage. Das Gebäude, das in deutlichem Kontrast zu seiner natürlichen Umgebung steht, besteht aus Materialien, die sein modernes Erscheinungsbild unterstreichen - neben Beton wurden auch Glas und Stahl ausgiebig eingesetzt. Die innovative „L"-Form bietet viel Platz für eine flexible Innenraumgestaltung. Im Erdgeschoss befindet sich ein großer, doppelhoch verglaster Wohnbereich, der im Kontrast zum Obergeschoss steht, das in seiner Betonhülle sehr komfortable Räume zur privaten Nutzung beherbergt. Große Stahllamellen durchqueren die Struktur in ihrem zentralen Teil und verbinden die beiden Stockwerke. Alle Räume sind dank der raumhohen Fenster mit natürlichem Licht durchflutet. Diese Glaselemente, die eine Verbindung nach außen herstellen, bilden auch einen markanten optischen Kontrast zu den massiven Materialien.

Côté rue, la Villa NEO, bâtie en béton brut, se présente comme une intersection solide et compacte de modules cubiques. Côté forêt, au contraire, la villa offre un aspect complètement différent avec des lignes sculpturales qui épousent de façon originale la topographie du terrain et ouvrent la vue sur le paysage densément boisé. Résolument contemporaine, la résidence repousse les limites du genre et remet en question le concept traditionnel de villa. Le bâtiment, qui tranche clairement avec son environnement naturel, est fait de matériaux qui soulignent son aspect moderne – en plus du béton, le verre et l'acier ont été largement utilisés. La forme novatrice en « L » offre beaucoup d'espace pour des arrangements intérieurs modulables. Le rez-de-chaussée comprend un grand espace de séjour vitré à double hauteur qui contraste avec l'étage supérieur qui, dans sa coque de béton, accueille des pièces d'usage privé très confortables. De grandes lames en acier traversent la structure dans sa partie centrale et relient les deux étages. Toutes les pièces sont inondées de lumière naturelle grâce à des fenêtres qui vont du sol au plafond. Ces éléments vitrés, qui font le lien avec l'extérieur, créent également un contraste visuel saisissant avec les matériaux solides.

ARCHITECTS: QUERKOPF ARCHITEKTEN /// **COMPLETION:** 2019 /// **FLOOR AREA:** 403 M² (4,338 FT²) /// **PHOTOS:** FRANK LÖSCHKE

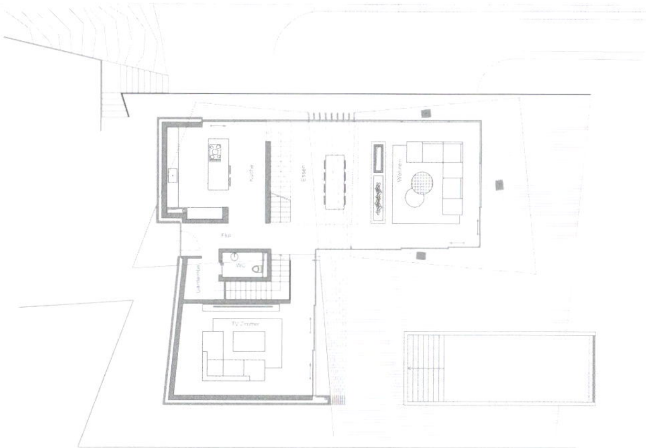

Façade opening up towards the garden

Fassade an der Gartenseite

Façade côté jardin

Ground floor plan

Grundriss Erdgeschosses

Plan du rez-de-chaussée

Living and dining area

Wohn- und Esszimmer

Salon et salle à manger

Interiors on the first floor

Innenräume (Obergeschoss)

Intérieurs (premier étage)

ARCHITECTS: PIETRIARCHITECTES /// **COMPLETION:** 2017 /// **FLOOR AREA:** 296 M^2 (3,186 FT^2) /// **PHOTOS:** PHILIPPE BIOLATTO

MAISON P

LE PUY-SAINTE-RÉPARADE, FRANCE

Cosily nestled on a hillside, MaisonP offers spectacular views of the Alps. The horizontal structure, despite its distinctive geometric shape, does not dominate over the landscape. On the contrary, the architecture's simple volumes emphasise the plateau of the spacious plot. The intervention into the dense vegetation on the parcel was minimal to preserve the wild and natural character of the site. MaisonP is an interesting structure, composed around empty spaces. A sculptural volume with numerous openings links the interiors to the surroundings. It comprises two parts: one-level house and an outbuilding. The first one is divided into the two separate volumes of the kitchen/dining area, and the bedroom/living space. The volumes are placed parallel and divided by a canal filled with plants and an interior pond. The entrance leads through this central part, which also filters natural light. The interiors are thus lit from all possible sides. However, to limit the surplus of sun, both parts are covered with flat and extensive roofs that create shaded outdoor spaces. The additional outbuilding located on the north-west part of the plot is slightly higher than the house itself. It houses the garage.

An einem Hang gelegen, bietet MaisonP eine spektakuläre Aussicht auf die Alpen. Trotz ihrer sehr individuellen geometrischen Form dominiert die Villa nicht die Landschaft. Im Gegenteil, ihre schlanke horizontale Struktur unterstreicht das ausgedehnte Plateau, auf dem die Villa gebaut ist. Die dichte Vegetation um das Haus herum wurde so weit wie möglich erhalten, um den wilden und natürlichen Charakter des Ortes zu bewahren. Die Struktur von MaisonP ist um leere Räume herum organisiert; sie erinnert an eine Skulptur. Die Villa hat viele Öffnungen, die das Innere mit der umgebenden Natur verbinden. Sie besteht aus zwei Teilen: einem einstöckigen Haus und einem Nebengebäude. Der erste ist in zwei getrennte Flügel unterteilt. In einem befinden sich die Küche und das Esszimmer, im anderen Schlaf- und Wohnzimmer. Diese parallel gebauten Bereiche sind durch ein kleines rechteckiges, mit Pflanzen verziertes Becken getrennt. Der Eingang befindet sich in diesem zentralen Teil, der die beiden Flügel verbindet und das natürliche Licht filtert. Das Innere der Villa wird so von allen Seiten beleuchtet. Aus Schutz vor der starken Sonne, sind beide Flächen mit überhängenden Flachdächern abgedeckt, die schattige Außenräume schaffen. Das im nordwestlichen Teil des Geländes gelegene Nebengebäude, in dem sich eine Garage befindet, ist etwas höher als das Haus selbst.

Confortablement nichée à flanc de colline, la MaisonP offre une vue spectaculaire sur les Alpes. Malgré sa forme géométrique très originale, la villa ne domine pas le paysage. Au contraire, sa structure horizontale aux lignes épurées met en valeur le plateau étendu sur lequel la villa est construite. La végétation dense autour de la maison a été préservée au maximum pour conserver le caractère sauvage et naturel du site. La structure de la MaisonP s'organise autour d'espaces vides ; elle fait penser à une sculpture. La villa dispose de nombreuses ouvertures reliant l'intérieur à la nature environnante. Elle se compose de deux parties : une maison de plain-pied et une dépendance. La première est divisée en deux ailes séparées, l'une avec la cuisine-salle à manger, l'autre avec la chambre à coucher et le séjour. Ces deux ailes sont construites parallèlement et séparées par un petit bassin rectangulaire décoré de plantes. L'entrée principale est située dans cette partie centrale qui relie les deux ailes et filtre la lumière naturelle. L'intérieur de la villa est ainsi éclairé de tous les côtés. Toutefois, pour limiter le surplus de soleil, les deux ailes sont couvertes par des toits plats qui créent des espaces extérieurs ombragés. Située dans la partie nord-ouest du terrain, la dépendance, qui abrite un garage, est légèrement plus haute que la maison elle-même.

Exterior view Außenansicht Vue extérieure

Central part Zentraler Bereich Partie centrale

Interiors Innenräume Intérieurs

Terrace view

Blick auf die Terrasse

Vue sur la terrasse

THE HUG

PAROS, CYCLADES, GREECE

"To hug is to be intimate, to bond, to protect, to keep close, to fit tightly, to cherish", reflect the architects, who have explained that "this project was visualised as a realisation of this simple yet vital act, and was named accordingly". Situated in the idyllic scenery of the island of Paros in the Cyclades, the villa is envisioned as a complex of two smaller buildings with a central courtyard protected from the Aegean northern winds. The villa's twin volumes are embraced with the parametric wall. Only the outdoor space with an infinity pool in the middle opens towards the seashore. Interestingly, the plastered white walls of the buildings are visible only from the inner courtyard. To provide privacy, passers-by can see only fragments of their elevations. The entrance to this intimate complex is located at the highest point of the plot and tucked between the stone buttressing walls. Blending the buildings into the gentle slopes of the surrounding landscape was the architects' main goal, just like a contemporary interpretation of typical Cycladic architecture.

„Umarmen bedeutet sich nahe zu sein, sich verbunden zu fühlen, zu schützen, etwas zusammenzuhalten und zu schätzen", erklären die Architekten. „Dieses Projekt wurde als eine Verwirklichung dieses einfachen, aber lebenswichtigen Aktes ins Auge gefasst und entsprechend benannt", fügen sie hinzu. Es liegt in einer idyllischen Landschaft auf der Kykladeninsel Paros und besteht aus einem Komplex aus zwei kleinen Gebäuden mit einem zentralen, vor den Winden der Nordägäis geschützten Innenhof. Beide Teile der Villa sind von einer umlaufenden Mauer umgeben. Nur der Außenbereich mit einem Infinity-Schwimmbad in der Mitte öffnet sich zur Küste. Die weiß verputzten Wände der Gebäude sind nur vom Innenhof aus sichtbar. Um die Privatsphäre zu gewährleisten, können die Passanten nur Fragmente davon sehen. Der Eingang zu diesem geschützten Komplex befindet sich am höchsten Punkt des Grundstücks. Der Zugang ist zwischen den steinernen Stützmauern eingekeilt. Das Hauptziel der Architekten war es, die Gebäude in die sanfte, hügelige Landschaft einzubetten. Sie bieten somit eine zeitgenössische Version der traditionellen kykladischen Architektur.

« Enlacer, c'est être proche, se lier, protéger, garder auprès de soi, serrer fort, chérir », expliquent les architectes. « Ce projet a été envisagé comme une réalisation de cet acte simple mais vital et a été nommé en conséquence », ajoutent-ils. Située dans un paysage idyllique de l'île de Paros, dans les Cyclades, la villa est conçue comme un complexe de deux petits bâtiments avec une cour centrale protégée des vents du nord de la mer Égée. Les deux parties de la villa sont entourées d'un mur d'enceinte. Seul l'espace extérieur qui entoure une piscine à débordement s'ouvre sur le bord de mer. Il est intéressant de noter que les murs blancs crépis des bâtiments ne sont visibles que depuis la cour intérieure. Pour assurer l'intimité, les passants ne peuvent en voir que des fragments. L'entrée de ce complexe intimiste est située au point le plus élevé de la parcelle. L'accès est coincé entre les murs de soutènement en pierre. L'objectif principal des architectes était de fondre les bâtiments dans les pentes douces du paysage environnant. Ils offrent ainsi une version contemporaine de l'architecture typique des Cyclades.

Exterior view Außenansicht Vue extérieure

ARCHITECTS: REACT ARCHITECTS /// **COMPLETION:** 2017 /// **FURTHER PARTICIPANTS:** IOANNIS KOUZOUMIS (COLLABORATING ARCHITECT), CHRISTOS SMYRNIS (STRUCTURAL ENGINEERING), NIKOS CHRYSTOFYLLAKIS (MECHANICAL & ELECTRICAL ENGINEERING), IOANNIS VAGIAS (SITE SUPERVISION ARCHITECT) /// **FLOOR AREA:** 150 M² (1,615 FT²) /// **PHOTOS:** GEORGE MESSARITAKIS

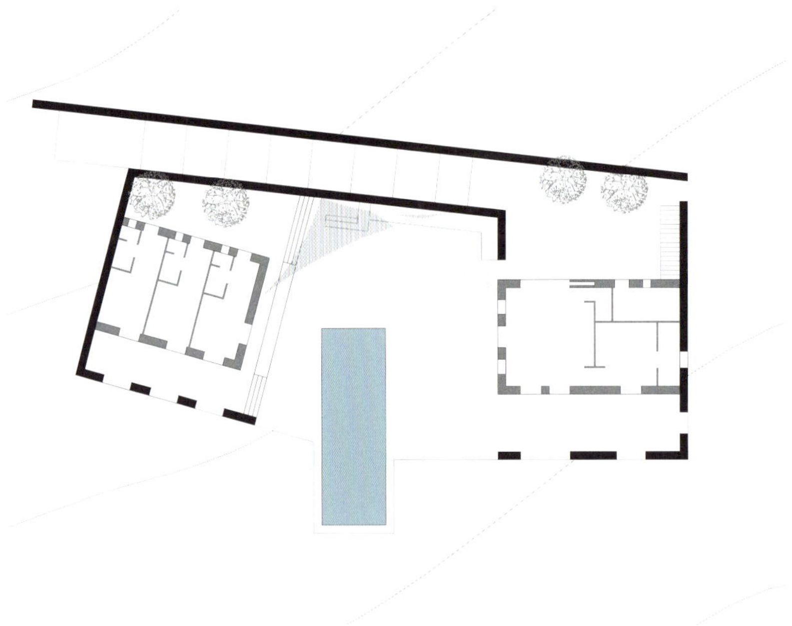

Main floor plan Gesamtplan Plan d'ensemble

Pool Swimmingpool Piscine

Exterior view Außenansicht Vue extérieure

Section Schnitt Section

Entrance Eingangsbereich Entrée

Terrace view

Blick auf die Terrasse

Vue sur la terrasse

CASA A

GUIMARÃES, PORTUGAL

CASA A is a beautifully choreographed space that balances voids with massive volumes. Located on the outskirts of Guimarães in a dense residential district, the house is adjusted to the topography and split into two floors. The architects' main concern was to design a structure that would provide privacy, which they achieved by carving into the terrain and using its height differences. The lower level, which from the top perspective seems to be sunk into the ground, embraces all the social areas. Numerous openings provide natural light, while the flexible scheme of fully opening window frames easily connects the interiors with an expansive outdoor area with a pool, as if they were one continuous space. This visual effect is enhanced by the use of similar colours and materials. The intriguing monolithic top volume, which is rotated in relation to the bottom silhouette, creates a cosy intimacy for all private spaces. Its outer shell is coated in wood, which counterbalances the chromatic greys of the concrete, a combination that is also used in the interiors. The house looks surprisingly different from the top and bottom parts of the plot.

CASA A ist ein wunderschönes Gebäude, das leere Räume mit massiven Elementen in Einklang bringt. Das Haus liegt am Stadtrand von Guimarães, in einem belebten Wohngebiet. Es ist der Topographie angepasst und auf zwei Etagen gebaut. Das Hauptanliegen der Architekten war es, ein Haus zu entwerfen, das eine gewisse Privatsphäre bietet. Zu diesem Zweck schnitten sie in das Gelände ein und nutzten die Höhenunterschiede. Von oben gesehen scheint das untere Stockwerk im Boden versenkt zu sein; es beherbergt alle Gemeinschaftsräume. Zahlreiche Fenster lassen natürliches Licht herein, während ein modulares System von vollständig zu öffnenden Fenstern einen bequemen Übergang zwischen den Innenräumen und dem großen Außenbereich mit Schwimmbad ermöglicht, als wäre es ein durchgehender Raum. Dieser Aspekt wird durch die Verwendung ähnlicher Farben und Materialien innen und außen verstärkt. Das Obergeschoss mit seiner monolithischen Form überlagert die Struktur des Untergeschosses in versetzter Weise. Dieser Versatz schafft in allen Räumen eine behagliche Atmosphäre. Die Außenhülle des Monolithen ist mit Holz verkleidet, was die Grautöne des Betons ausgleicht. Die gleiche Materialkombination findet sich auch in den Innenräumen. Das Haus sieht von oben und unten betrachtet völlig unterschiedlich aus.

La CASA A est un endroit magnifiquement aménagé qui concilie les espaces vides avec des éléments massifs. Située à la périphérie de Guimarães, dans un quartier résidentiel animé, la maison est adaptée à la topographie et construite sur deux étages. Le souci principal des architectes était de concevoir une maison qui offrirait une certaine intimité. Ils ont pour cela taillé dans le terrain et utilisé les différences de hauteur. Vu d'en haut, l'étage inférieur, qui accueille toutes les pièces communes, semble enfoncé dans le sol. De nombreuses baies vitrées laissent passer la lumière naturelle tandis qu'un système modulable de fenêtres à ouverture totale offre une transition aisée entre les espaces intérieurs et la grande aire extérieure équipée d'une piscine, comme s'il s'agissait d'un espace continu. Cet aspect est renforcé par l'utilisation de couleurs et de matériaux semblables au-dedans comme au-dehors. L'étage supérieur à l'étrange forme monolithique se superpose en décalé sur la structure de l'étage inférieur. Ce décalage crée une intimité douillette qui berce tous les espaces privés. L'enveloppe extérieure du monolithe est recouverte de bois afin de contrebalancer les nuances grises du béton. On retrouve la même combinaison de matériaux dans les intérieurs. La maison a un aspect totalement différent selon qu'on la regarde du haut ou du bas du terrain.

ARCHITECTS: REM'A /// **COMPLETION:** 2019 /// **FLOOR AREA:** 450M² (4,844 FT²) /// **PHOTOS :** IVO TAVARES STUDIO

Exterior view

Außenansicht

Vue extérieure

Terrace view

Blick auf die Terrasse

Vue sur la terrasse

Section Schnitt Section

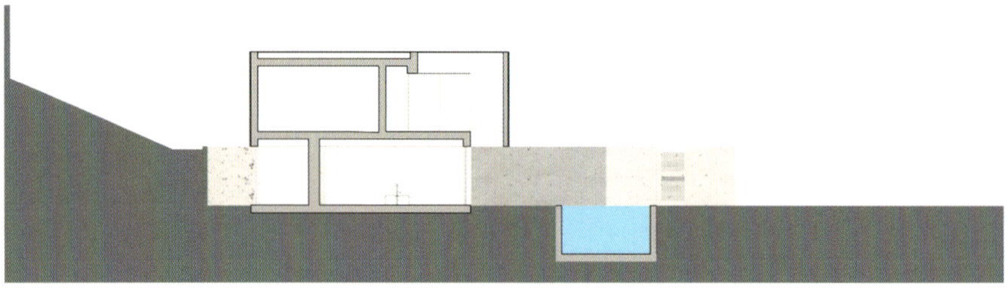

Interiors Innenräume Intérieurs

ARCHITECTS: ROB DUBOIS ARQUITECTE /// **COMPLETION:** 2018 /// **FURTHER PARTICIPANTS:** JORDI FONTANELLA (TECHNICAL ARCHITECT) /// **FLOOR AREA:** 300 M² (3,229 FT²) /// **PHOTOS:** JORDI MIRALLES

CASA BIELMANN – RIOS

SANTA MARIA DE PALAUTORDERA, SPAIN

A sloping plot near Barcelona became the scenic location for this structurally dramatic house, which is energy independent thanks to its geothermal and photovoltaic installation. A self-sufficient heating and cooling installation, as well as an electricity supply, was one of the clients' main wishes. The second was an entirely open and diaphanous ground floor. Based on a simple rectangular plan, the volume sits in parallel to the streets limiting the plot. This allows for panoramic views of the Montseny mountain range and the garden behind the house. The grounds are irrigated by rainwater, which is redirected from the roof to a special tank dug into the garden. On the eastern side, a monumental curtain wall made of black aluminium envelopes a double-high space facing the garden. On the ground floor, the architects used the maximum possible surface of glass for a smooth inside-outside connection. The open-space character of this level enhances juxtaposition of its lightness with the massiveness of the structural elements made of concrete, like the folded slab with overhangs covering the volume to protect it from overheating during the summer. The upper floor contains elements that ensure more privacy.

Casa Bielmann – Rios liegt malerisch auf einem abschüssigen Gelände in der Nähe von Barcelona. Der Standort ist ideal für das eindrucksvolle Haus. Dank seiner geothermischen und photovoltaischen Anlagen ist es energieunabhängig. Die Eigentümer wünschten sich insbesondere ein autonomes Heiz- und Kühlsystem sowie eine Stromversorgung aus natürlichen Energiequellen. Ausserdem sollte das Erdgeschoss vollkommen offen und transparent sein. Das nach einem einfachen rechteckigen Plan errichtete Gebäude verläuft parallel zu den angrenzenden Straßen. Diese Anordnung bietet einen Panoramablick auf die Montseny-Bergkette und den Garten hinter dem Haus. Letzterer wird mit Regenwasser bewässert, das vom Dach in einen speziellen, in den Garten gegrabenen Tank umgeleitet wird. Eine monumentale Vorhangfassade aus schwarzen Aluminiumprofilen an der Ostseite umschließt einen zweigeschossigen Raum zum Garten hin. Eine raumhohe Glasfront schafft im Erdgeschoss einen fließenden Übergang zwischen innen und außen und durchflutet den offenen Wohnraum mit Licht. Sie wird den massiveren Elementen der Betonstruktur gegenübergestellt. Die gefaltete Platte mit Überhängen, die das Gebäude abdeckt, schützt es vor Überhitzung im Sommer. Einige dekorative Elemente im Obergeschoss sorgen für mehr Privatsphäre.

Lieu pittoresque, ce terrain en pente près de Barcelone est l'emplacement idéal pour cette maison aux formes spectaculaires. Elle est énergétiquement indépendante grâce à ses installations géothermiques et photovoltaïques. Ce sont les propriétaires qui avaient souhaité disposer d'un système de chauffage et de refroidissement autonome ainsi que d'une source naturelle d'approvisionnement en électricité. Leur second souhait était que le rez-de-chaussée soit entièrement libre et transparent. Construit selon un plan rectangulaire simple, le bâtiment est parallèle aux rues mitoyennes. Cet arrangement offre une vue panoramique sur la chaîne de montagnes du Montseny et sur le jardin derrière la maison. Ce dernier est irrigué par l'eau de pluie qui est redirigée du toit vers un réservoir spécial creusé dans le jardin. Un mur-rideau monumental en profilés d'aluminium noir sur le côté est enveloppe un séjour sur deux étages qui fait face au jardin. Au rez-de-chaussée, les architectes ont utilisé la plus grande surface de verre possible pour un passage intérieur-extérieur harmonieux. Au rez-de-chaussée, conçu comme un espace ouvert, la luminosité provenant de l'extérieur domine. Elle est juxtaposée aux éléments plus massifs de la structure en béton. La dalle pliée avec des surplombs qui couvre le bâtiment le protège de la surchauffe pendant l'été. Certains éléments décoratifs à l'étage supérieur sont conçus pour offrir plus d'intimité.

Exterior view Außenansicht Vue extérieure

Terrace view

Blick auf die Terrasse

Vue sur la terrasse

Kitchen and dining area

Küche und Esszimmer

Cuisine et salle à manger

Staircase Escalier Treppe

Living room Wohnzimmer Salon

Interiors on the first floor

Innenräume (Obergeschoss)

Intérieurs (premier étage)

SINGLE-FAMILY HOUSE HA14

WANGEN, GERMANY

This curious composition of volumes is an inventive response to the plot's topography. The entrance to the house is on the narrow side, on the basement level, just next to the garage door. A staircase leads up to the living floor, which is located on a plateau above the street level. To benefit from the views, the walls open along the length of the building toward the south. The wooden outdoor terrace fluidly links the house with the garden. In addition to the residential part, HA14 also includes a small office and a lounge for "entrepreneurial visions", which is located in the long overhang volume sitting on the very top. On the entrance side it has access to a roof terrace, and on the opposite side, to the second floor of the house with private rooms. The interiors echo this unconventional structure as well as the rising terrain – to make the cantilever possible, the kitchen below is lower. The dining area, by contrast, is a two-storey high space, while the living room has a regular one-level height. Each space has a distinctive character.

Die ungewöhnliche Anordnung der verschiedenen Teile dieser Villa ist eine innovative Lösung für die Topographie des Landes. Der Eingang befindet sich am schmalen Hang, direkt neben dem Garagentor im Kellergeschoss. Eine Treppe führt zu den Wohnräumen, die sich auf einem Plateau hoch über der Straße befinden. Um die Aussicht zu genießen, öffnen sich die Wände über die gesamte Länge des Gebäudes nach Süden. Eine Außenterrasse aus Holz bietet einen harmonischen Übergang zwischen Haus und Garten. Neben dem Wohnteil umfasst die Villa HA14 auch ein kleines Büro und ein Wohnzimmer mit Panoramablick, um den „unternehmerischen Weitblick" zu fördern. Letzteres befindet sich in dem lang auskragenden Gebäude an der Spitze der Konstruktion. Eine Glastür gibt Zugang zu einer Dachterrasse über dem ersten Stock. Die Privatzimmer befinden sich auf der anderen Seite des zweiten Stocks. Die Innenräume sind sowohl an diese ungewöhnliche Struktur als auch an den schrägen Boden angepasst. Um die Auskragung über den schrägen Boden zu bauen, hat die darunter liegende Küche eine niedrigere Decke als der Rest. Das Esszimmer hingegen ist ein zweistöckiger Raum, während das Wohnzimmer eine normale Höhe hat. Alle Räume sind in einem unterschiedlichen Stil dekoriert.

La curieuse disposition des différentes parties de la villa constitue une solution originale à la topographie du terrain. La porte d'entrée se trouve sur le versant étroit, juste à côté du garage au sous-sol. Un escalier mène aux pièces d'habitation situées sur un plateau surélevé par rapport à la rue. Pour profiter de la vue les murs s'ouvrent sur toute la longueur du bâtiment vers le sud. Une terrasse extérieure en bois offre une transition harmonieuse entre la maison et le jardin. En plus de la partie résidentielle, la villa HA14 comprend également un petit bureau et un salon avec vue panoramique pour stimuler la « clairvoyance entrepreneuriale ». Ce dernier est situé dans le long bâtiment en surplomb tout en haut de la construction. Une porte vitrée donne accès à une terrasse sur le toit du premier étage. Les appartements privés se trouvent de l'autre côté du deuxième étage. Les intérieurs sont adaptés à cette structure insolite aussi qu'au terrain en pente ; pour édifier le bâtiment en porte-à-faux sur cette parcelle inclinée, la cuisine en dessous a un plafond plus bas que le reste. La salle à manger, au contraire, est un espace de deux étages, tandis que le salon a une hauteur de plafond normale. Toutes les pièces sont décorées dans un style différent.

Entrance Eingangsbereich Entrée

Exterior view Außenansicht Vue extérieure

ARCHITECTS: SCHILLER ARCHITEKTUR BDA /// **COMPLETION:** 2015 /// **FLOOR AREA:** 460 M² (4,951 FT²) /// **PHOTOS:** RONALD TILLEMAN

Interiors Innenräume Intérieurs

TINEL

ŽRNOVO, KORČULA ISLAND, CROATIA

This breathtaking structure was envisioned for the dramatic landscape of its north-oriented slope. While respecting the heritage values of the local buildings, like simplicity, functionality, and human scale, the architects designed spaces that would also reflect a contemporary way of life. The relatively small yet steep and narrow plot inspired them to create a structure that would be completely incorporated into the hill. The result is a semi-underground twin house realised as a compilation of volumes with a luxurious flair. The spatial relations between the inside and outside were crucial for this project, which is why numerous walls were given floor-to-ceiling glass windows and all flat roofs of the sculpturous structure act as terraces. These external surfaces are maximised to provide as much space for outdoor activities as possible, to align with with the Mediterranean lifestyle. Despite the complexity of the shape, the terraces on different levels are fluidly connected with each other through stairs and are easily accessible from the interiors. In particular, the main terrace with the pool on the very top defines the relaxed ambiance of the house and offers stunning views. The original shape of the twin house somehow resembles binoculars.

Dieses atemberaubende, an einem Nordhang gelegene Gebäude wurde ganz im Bewusstsein seiner beeindruckenden Landschaft entworfen. Unter Berücksichtigung lokaler Bautraditionen wie Einfachheit und Funktionalität konzipierten die Architekten Räumlichkeiten, die einen zeitgenössischen Lebensstil widerspiegeln und sich bestens dafür eignen. Das relativ kleine, steile und schmale Grundstück hat die Umrisse dieser Villa bestimmt, sodass sie mit ihrer Umgebung verschmilzt. Sie besteht aus einem Doppelhaus mit Souterrains und luxuriösen Räumen, die übereinander angeordnet sind. Die Beziehung zwischen innen und außen ist ein entscheidendes Element dieses Projekts: Die meisten Wände haben raumhohe Fenster, und alle Flachdächer des Gebäudes fungieren als Terrassen. Diese Außenflächen sind äußerst großzügig bemessen, um im Einklang mit dem mediterranen Lebensstil möglichst viel Platz für Aktivitäten im Freien zu bieten. Trotz der komplexen Bauweise sind die verschiedenen Ebenen mit Terrassen durch Treppen fließend miteinander verbunden und von innen leicht zugänglich. Insbesondere die Hauptterrasse spiegelt zusammen mit dem Swimmingpool die entspannte Atmosphäre des Hauses wider und bietet eine atemberaubende Aussicht. Die ursprüngliche Form des Hauses, in Form eines Fernglases, unterstreicht die Bedeutung, die dem Panorama beigemessen wird.

Cet édifice aux formes audacieuses a été conçu pour mettre en valeur le paysage spectaculaire qui s'offre sur cette colline orientée vers le nord. Tout en respectant les valeurs traditionnelles de l'architecture locale telles que la simplicité, la fonctionnalité ou la dimension humaine des bâtiments, les architectes ont conçu des espaces qui s'adaptent parfaitement au mode de vie contemporain. Le terrain relativement petit, raide et étroit a déterminé les contours de cette villa qui semble intégrée à la colline. Elle se présente sous la forme de deux maisons siamoises à moitié enterrées. Les parties du bâtiment, à l'aspect luxueux, sont superposées. La relation entre l'intérieur et l'extérieur est un élément crucial de ce projet : la plupart des murs sont équipés de fenêtres du sol au plafond et tous les toits plats de la structure font office de terrasses. Ces surfaces extérieures sont utilisées au maximum pour offrir le plus d'espace possible aux activités de plein air selon le mode de vie méditerranéen. Malgré la complexité des formes, les terrasses des différents étages sont bien reliées entre elles par des escaliers et facilement accessibles depuis l'intérieur. La terrasse supérieure, avec la piscine, reflète l'ambiance détendue de la maison et offre une vue imprenable. La forme originale de la maison, en forme de jumelles, souligne encore l'importance accordée au panorama.

ARCHITECTS: SODAA /// **COMPLETION:** 2017 /// **FURTHER PARTICIPANTS:** VEDRAN JUKIĆ (MAIN ARCHITECT), MAŠA MEDOŠ (COLLABORATION), MIHAELA GOLUŽA, JURE ČUDINA (PROJECT TEAM) /// **FLOOR AREA:** 2 X 240 M^2 (5,167 FT^2) /// **PHOTOS:** DAVOR RADMAN (DRONE), MARKO MIHALJEVIC

General view Gesamtansicht Vue générale

Terrace view

Blick auf die Terrasse

Vue sur la terrasse

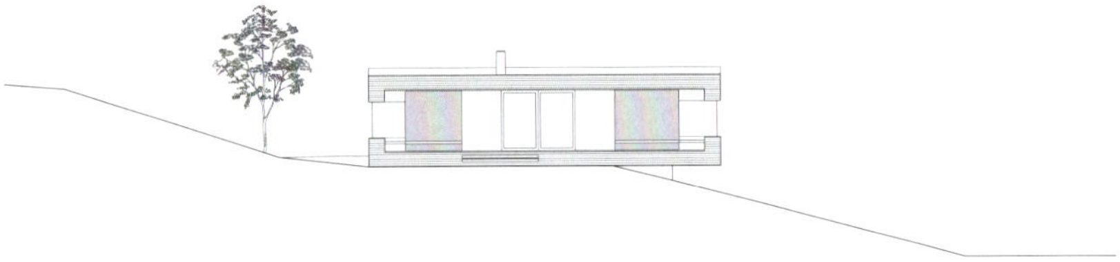

Façade opening up towards the garden

Fassade an der Gartenseite

Façade côté jardin

Ground floor plan

Grundriss Erdgeschoss

Plan du rez-de-chaussée

ARCHITECTS: SUPER FUTURE GROUP / ROBERT LAMPRECHT /// **COMPLETION:** 2019 /// **FLOOR AREA:** 346 M² (3,724 FT²) /// **PHOTOS:** SIMON OBERHOFER

VILLA MARIE

KREMSMÜNSTER, AUSTRIA

Villa Marie is based on a bungalow concept with all rooms organised around the central living area on one level. The focus, however, is on the extremely spacious veranda oriented to the west. As a link between the living room and the garden, the terrace is covered and offers a cosy outdoor space. The villa is located at the hilly foot of the Alps, and this original social area is also perfect for enjoying the spectacular view. Thanks to a large void in the middle of the roof and a huge sliding door between the inside and outside, the interiors are filled with ample natural light. The living area is defined by three volumes, each of which has a different function – the kitchen area, the fireplace and seating area, and the cabinets and storage space. These areas are arranged as an open spatial continuum, with no doors visible from the main living room. Interestingly, on the south side the structure levitates over the slope, which camouflages the entrance and service level in the basement. The wooden construction of the villa is fully prefabricated and assembled on site.

Die Villa Marie ist nach dem Bungalow-Konzept gebaut: alle Räume befinden sich auf einer Etage und sind um ein zentrales Wohnzimmer herum organisiert. Der Schwerpunkt liegt hier jedoch auf der geräumigen Veranda, die nach Westen ausgerichtet ist. Diese Verandaterrasse verbindet das Wohnzimmer mit dem Garten: Sie ist teilweise überdacht und bietet einen komfortablen Außenbereich. Da die Villa im Voralpenland liegt, dient die Terrasse als Gemeinschaftsraum. Es ist auch so eingerichtet, dass man den herrlichen Ausblick genießen kann. Ein großer Ausschnitt in der Mitte des Daches und eine riesige Schiebetür zwischen innen und außen sorgen für natürliches Licht in den Innenräumen. Das Wohnzimmer ist in drei Teile unterteilt, die jeweils eine unterschiedliche Funktion haben: die Küchenecke, der Kamin und die Sitzecke sowie die Schränke und der Stauraum. Diese drei Teile sind als ein durchgehender offener Raum angeordnet, ohne Türen, die vom Herzen des Raumes aus sichtbar wären. Eine weitere charakteristische Eigenschaft ist, dass das Bauwerk auf der Südseite auf dem Hang zu schweben scheint, was es ermöglicht, den Eingang und die Servicetage im Untergeschoss zu tarnen. Die Holzkonstruktion der Villa ist vollständig vorgefertigt und wurde vor Ort montiert.

La Villa Marie est construite selon le concept des bungalows : toutes les pièces sont situées sur un étage et organisées autour d'une salle de séjour centrale. Cependant, l'accent est plutôt mis ici sur la véranda spacieuse orientée plein ouest. Cette terrasse-véranda fait le lien entre le séjour et le jardin : elle est en partie couverte et offre un espace extérieur confortable. Comme la villa est située au pied des Alpes, la terrasse fait office de pièce commune. Elle est d'ailleurs arrangée pour qu'on puisse profiter de la vue magnifique. Un grand espace découpé au milieu du toit et une énorme porte coulissante entre l'intérieur et l'extérieur procurent de la lumière naturelle aux intérieurs. La salle de séjour est divisée en trois parties dont chacune a une fonction différente : le coin cuisine, la cheminée et le coin salon, ainsi que les armoires et les rangements. Ces trois parties sont disposées comme un espace ouvert et continu, sans portes qui seraient visibles depuis le cœur de la pièce. Autre spécificité notoire, la structure semble léviter sur la pente du côté sud, ce qui permet de camoufler l'entrée et l'étage de service au sous-sol. La construction en bois de la villa est entièrement préfabriquée et a été assemblée sur place.

Street façade

Straßenansicht

Façade côté rue

Terrace view

Blick auf die Terrasse

Vue sur la terrasse

Interiors Innenräume Intérieurs

ARCHITECTS: SCHAMP & SCHMALÖER ARCHITEKTEN STADTPLANER PARTGMBB /// **COMPLETION:** 2016 /// **FURTHER PARTICIPANTS:** BUERO N, HELLMUT NEIDHARDT (LANDSCAPE PLANNING) /// **FLOOR AREA:** 190 M² (2,045 FT²) /// **PHOTOS:** HANS-JÜRGEN LANDES

Street façade

Fassade an der Straßenseite

Façade côté rue

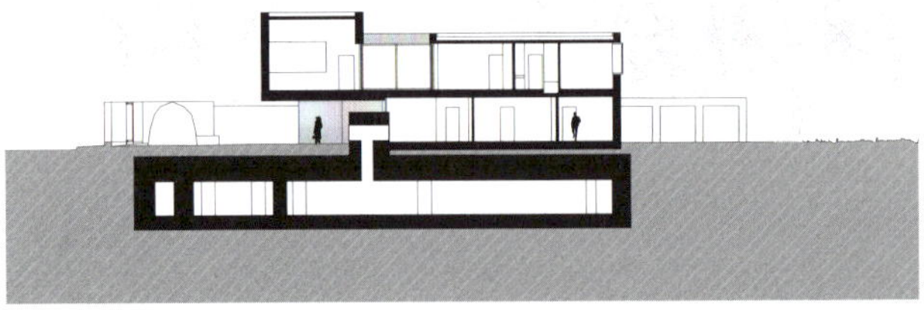

Section Schnitt Section

HOUSE S7

DORTMUND, GERMANY

Entrance Eingangsbereich Entrée

The light structure of House S7 is based on the solid foundation of a former air-raid shelter. There are still three above-ground entrances to the bunker, one of which was integrated into the ground floor plan. As the house sits at the edge of a city district and faces a highly frequented foot and bicycle path, the architects invented a structural solution to provide the owners with some privacy. A 16-meter-long lamella wall made of perforated sheets reminiscent of a Moorish style elegantly protects residents from the eyes of passers-by but can also be fully opened in case the inhabitants wish to enjoy vistas of the neighbourhood. Behind this view-filtering screen there is a spacious and partly covered patio, which effectively extends the living area inside the house through a set of large folding windows. The side elevations of the house are more compact. The entrance façade is suspended and thus creates a roofed space for parking the car. On the opposite side, the cantilevered corner window highlighted against the delicate brick surface is a visual continuation of the lamella structure and offers yet another way to enjoy the views of the surroundings.

Die leichte Struktur des S7-Hauses ist auf den massiven Fundamenten eines ehemaligen Luftschutzbunkers gebaut. Es gab drei ebenerdige Eingänge zum Bunker; einer davon wurde in den Grundriss des Erdgeschosses integriert. Da sich das Haus in der Nähe des Stadtteilzentrums befindet und auf einen stark befahrenen Fahrrad- und Fußgängerweg blickt, haben die Architekten eine Baulösung gefunden, die den Eigentümern ein gewisses Maß an Privatsphäre bietet. Eine 16-Meter-lange Lamellenwand aus Lochblech im maurischen Stil schützt sie wirksam vor dem Blick auf den Weg; die Wand kann jedoch vollständig geöffnet werden, wenn die Bewohner die Aussicht auf die Nachbarschaft genießen möchten. Hinter der Wand verbirgt sich ein geräumiger, teilweise überdachter Innenhof, der dank großer Faltfenster den Wohnraum des Hauses wirkungsvoll erweitert. Die Seiten des Hauses sind kompakter. Die Vorderseite des Eingangs ist freitragend, wodurch ein überdachter Platz zum Abstellen des Autos geschaffen wird. Am anderen Ende erweitert ein auskragendes, in die Ziegelfläche eingelassenes Eckfenster den Raum optisch und bietet eine weitere Gelegenheit, den Blick auf die Umgebung zu bewundern.

La structure légère de la maison S7 est construite sur les fondations massives d'un ancien abri antiaérien. Il restait trois entrées de plain-pied qui donnait accès au bunker ; l'une a été intégrée au plan du rez-de-chaussée. Comme la maison se trouve près du cœur d'un quartier animé et donne sur une piste cyclable et piétonne très fréquentée, les architectes ont inventé une méthode de construction qui offre aux propriétaires une certaine intimité. Un mur à lamelles de 16 mètres de long, fait de tôles perforées de style mauresque, les protège efficacement des regards du chemin ; ce mur peut cependant être entièrement ouvert lorsque les habitants souhaitent profiter de la vue sur le quartier. Le mur cache un patio spacieux et partiellement couvert qui prolonge avec bonheur l'espace de séjour de la maison grâce à de grandes fenêtres en accordéon. Les parties latérales de la maison sont plus compactes. La façade où se trouve l'entrée est en porte-à-faux et crée ainsi un espace couvert pour le stationnement de la voiture. À l'autre bout, une fenêtre d'angle saillante encastrée dans la surface en briques prolonge visuellement la structure à lamelles ; elle offre une occasion de plus d'admirer la vue sur les environs.

Patio Innenhof Patio

Interiors Innenräume Intérieurs

Terrace view on the ground floor

Blick auf die Terrasse im Erdgeschoss

Vue sur la terrasse du rez-de-chaussée

Exterior view with the bunker entrance

Außenansicht mit Bunkereingang

Vue extérieure avec l'entrée du bunker

ARCHITECTS: TETRO ARQUITETURA /// **COMPLETION:** 2016 /// **FLOOR AREA:** 300 M² (3,229 FT²) /// **PHOTOS:** AUGUSTO CUSTÓDIO, JOMAR BRAGANÇA

General view Gesamtansicht Vue générale

INCLINED SLAB HOUSE

NOVA LIMA, BRAZIL

Inclined Slab House is set amidst the scenery of steep slopes covered with Brazilian savanna vegetation. This exciting topography inspired the unconventional shape of the residence, adjusted to the longitudinal plot and evolving down the hill. Made of concrete slab, which fluidly merges the architecture with the landscape, the structure is covered by a wooden roof deck for thermal comfort. The spectacular roof top pool offers plenty of sun and panoramic vistas. A couple of trees planted next to the water are a source of shade and refreshing breezes. The connected living and dining areas are located just below the roof slab, which filters natural light. On the opposite side, a 12-metre single panel glass door on a steel frame connects the living room with the courtyard, surrounded by a stone retaining wall. The striking transparency in the structure creates a visual effect as if the living room were a large balcony. All private spaces below the ground floor also have generously glazed walls and thus offer views of the dramatic natural setting. The architects achieved a successful balance between the solid and distinctive structure and a dialogue with the surroundings.

Das Inclined Slab House befindet sich an einem steilen, bewachsenen Hang im Herzen der brasilianischen Savanne. Diese besondere Topografie inspirierte die ungewöhnliche Form dieses Hauses, die sich an das Längsgrundstück anpasst und das sich am Fuße des Hügels verbreitert. Eine riesige, das Bauwerk dominierende Betonplatte mit einem wärmeregulierenden Holzdach schmiegt sich so in das Relief, dass das Haus mit der Landschaft verschmilzt. Der spektakuläre Pool auf dem Dach bietet viel Sonnenschein und eine atemberaubende Aussicht auf die Umgebung. Einige wenige Bäume neben dem Pool spenden Schatten und sorgen für eine frische Brise. Wohn- und Esszimmer sind miteinander verbunden und befinden sich direkt unter der Dachplatte, sodass natürliches Licht einfallen kann. Auf der gegenüberliegenden Seite verbindet eine 12 Meter lange, einteilige Glastür auf einem Stahlrahmen das Wohnzimmer mit dem Innenhof, der von einer steinernen Stützmauer umgeben ist. Die extreme Transparenz der Bauweise erzeugt einen optischen Effekt: Das Wohnzimmer wirkt wie ein großer Balkon. Alle Räume unter dem Erdgeschoss haben ebenfalls große Glaswände und öffnen sich zur umgebenden Natur. Den Architekten ist es gelungen, das Gleichgewicht zwischen einer sehr originellen, massiven Struktur und dem Dialog mit der Natur zu wahren.

Inclined Slab House est située sur une pente raide et couverte de végétation au cœur de la savane brésilienne. Cette topographie étonnante a inspiré la forme insolite de cette résidence adaptée à la parcelle longitudinale sur laquelle elle est bâtie et qui s'élargit au bas de la colline. Une immense dalle de béton, qui épouse le relief et fait ainsi fondre la maison dans le paysage, domine la structure. Cette dalle est couverte d'un toit en bois pour plus de confort thermique. Une piscine panoramique sur le toit est baignée de soleil et offre une vue imprenable sur les alentours. Quelques arbres plantés à côté du bassin sont une source d'ombre et de brise appréciable. La salle de séjour et la salle à manger, reliées entre elles, se trouvent juste en-dessous de la dalle du toit ce qui permet de filtrer la lumière naturelle. Du côté opposé, une porte vitrée à simple panneau de 12 mètres posée sur un cadre en acier relie le salon à la cour. Cette dernière est entourée d'un mur de soutènement en pierre. L'extrême transparence du panneau de verre crée un effet d'optique : le salon prend ainsi des airs de grand balcon. Toutes les chambres situées sous le rez-de-chaussée sont elles aussi équipées de grands murs vitrés et s'ouvrent ainsi sur la nature environnante. Les architectes sont parvenus à conserver l'équilibre entre une structure massive très originale et le souci de respecter l'environnement.

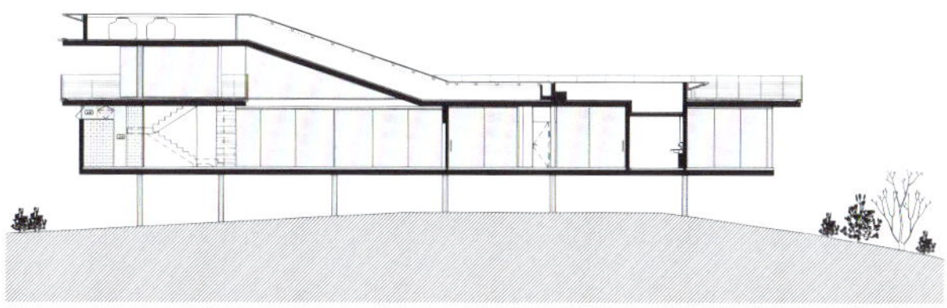

Living and dining area

Wohn- und Esszimmer

Salon et salle à manger

Patio

Section Schnitt Section

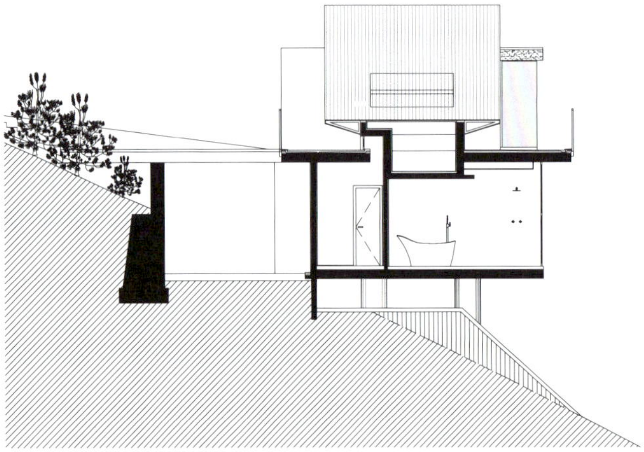

Interiors Innenräume Intérieurs

Section Schnitt Section

GAFARIM HOUSE

PONTE DE LIMA, PORTUGAL

Gafarim House is a beautiful play of pure geometry juxtaposed with its natural environment. Its design theme is contradictions and oppositions – contemporary versus vernacular, transparent versus opaque, light versus massive, and open plane versus blind volume. Sitting in the middle of a mountainous landscape, it is quite a monolithic volume. From the street side, the façade is compact and closed. The composition of shapes, distinctive through their white colour, is an intriguing introduction to the extensive structure hidden behind protective walls. A small entrance expands to a double-height volume that houses the social functions of the house and combines the kitchen, dining, and living areas. This part of the house was given a generous glass wall offering an unobstructed view of the garden, up to the horizon line. The extensive outdoor terrace with a pool is the interconnection between the interior and the grounds. Without any distinctive separation, the private spaces of the house are located in the volume facing towards the southeast. One of the innovative elements is a small interior patio, serving both the master bedroom and bathroom.

Haus Gafarim ist ein kleines Juwel der reinen Geometrie in einer natürlichen Umgebung. Die Themen, die den Ausschlag für die Gestaltung gaben, sind Widersprüche und Gegensätze: Moderne versus Tradition, Transparenz versus Undurchsichtigkeit, Leichtigkeit versus Massivität, offene Räume versus blinde Wände. Im Herzen einer Berglandschaft gelegen, ist es ein eher monolithisches Ensemble. Auf der Straßenseite ist die Fassade kompakt und geschlossen. Der Aufbau ihrer auffälligen, weiß gestrichenen geometrischen Formen lässt die großzügige Struktur hinter den Schutzmauern erahnen. Die kleine Eingangshalle weicht schnell einem großen Raum von doppelter Höhe, der als Empfangsraum dient und Küche, Esszimmer und Wohnzimmer zusammenführt. Dieser Teil des Hauses hat eine riesige Glaswand, die einen ungehinderten Blick auf den Garten ermöglicht, dessen Grenzen sich am Horizont verlieren. Eine große Außenterrasse mit Swimmingpool bildet einen Übergang zwischen der Villa und dem Garten. Ohne besondere Trennung von den anderen Räumen befinden sich die privaten Bereiche des Hauses im süd-östlichen Teil. Ein kleiner Innenpatio, der sowohl an das Hauptschlafzimmer als auch an das Bad grenzt, ist ein weiteres Merkmal dieser Villa.

La maison Gafarim est un petit bijou de géométrie pure dans un écrin de nature. Les thèmes qui ont présidé à sa conception sont les contradictions et les oppositions : modernité contre tradition, transparence et opacité, légèreté et épaisseur, espaces ouverts contre murs aveugles. Située au cœur d'un paysage montagneux, c'est un ensemble assez monolithique. Côté rue, la façade est compacte et fermée. La juxtaposition de formes géométriques qui la composent, toutes peintes en blanc, laisse cependant imaginer les grands espaces intérieurs cachés derrière ces murs protecteurs. Le petit hall d'entrée cède rapidement la place à un grand espace de hauteur double qui sert de pièce de réception et réunit la cuisine, la salle à manger et le salon. Cette partie de la maison est dotée d'un immense mur de verre qui offre une vue dégagée sur le jardin dont l'étendue se perd à l'horizon. Une grande terrasse extérieure avec piscine fait le lien entre la villa et le jardin. Sans aucune séparation particulière des autres pièces, les appartements privés de la maison sont situés dans la partie orientée vers le sud-est. Un petit patio intérieur qui dessert à la fois la chambre principale et la salle de bains est une autre caractéristique de cette villa.

ARCHITECTS: TIAGO DO VALE ARCHITECTS /// **COMPLETION:** 2018 /// **FLOOR AREA:** 1070 M² (11,517 FT²) /// **PHOTOS:** JOÃO MORGADO

Exterior view Außenansicht Vue extérieure

Living and dining area

Wohn- und Esszimmer

Salon et salle à manger

Terrace view

Blick auf die Terrasse

Vue sur la terrasse

MONOLITHISCHES ENSEMBLE

PLANEGG, GERMANY

A sculptural ensemble of two orthogonal structures creates interesting visual effects, which change depending on the perspective and the path of the sun. The exterior walls built of light concrete enhance the monolithic character of both volumes. The homogenous style continues in the interiors, where exposed concrete is combined with white walls and wooden floors to create a minimal yet elegant look. All openings are planned to let the maximum amount of natural light inside, while minimalizing the views from the outside. The interiors are thus a well-balanced juxtaposition between glazed and solid surfaces. The heart of the main house is the living space, on the ground floor, with the dining area smoothly connected to an outdoor terrace through a large glass wall that continues into a green garden, hidden from the street perspective. The lower and simplified volume of the guest house is a smaller scale with the same solutions. Slightly distanced to the side of the plot, it also opens onto the common garden area. While both buildings are heated with a groundwater heat pump, their roofs are extensively greened.

Diese elegante Gegenüberstellung zweier orthogonaler Strukturen erzeugt einen interessanten optischen Effekt: Das Aussehen der Villa ändert sich je nach Blickwinkel und Sonnenverlauf. Die aus Infraleichtbeton gebauten Außenwände unterstreichen den monolithischen Eindruck, der von beiden Gebäuden ausgeht. Derselbe einheitliche Stil ist auch im Inneren zu finden, wo Sichtbeton mit weißen

Wänden und Holzböden kombiniert und ein minimalistisches, aber dennoch raffiniertes Erscheinungsbild erzeugt. Alle Öffnungen sind so gestaltet, dass sie ein Maximum an natürlichem Licht hereinlassen und gleichzeitig die Sicht von außen einschränken. Die Innenräume bilden so ein ausgewogenes Ensemble zwischen Glas und massiven Flächen. Das Wohnzimmer im Erdgeschoss ist zusammen mit dem Esszimmer das Herzstück des Haupthauses. Letzteres ist durch eine große Glaswand mit der Terrasse verbunden. Ein von der Straßenansicht verborgener Garten erweitert die Perspektive. Das Gästehaus, niedriger und einfacher gebaut, bietet den gleichen Aspekt in kleinerem Maßstab. Am Rande des Grundstücks gelegen, öffnet es sich auch zum Garten hin. Beide Gebäude werden mit einer Grundwasser-Wärmepumpe beheizt und ihre Dächer sind extensiv begrünt.

Cette élégante juxtaposition de deux structures orthogonales crée un effet optique intéressant : l'aspect de la villa change en fonction du point de vue et de la trajectoire du soleil. Les murs extérieurs, construits en béton léger, accentuent l'impression monolithique qui se dégage des deux parties. On retrouve le même style épuré à l'intérieur où le béton apparent s'harmonise avec des murs blancs et des planchers en bois pour créer un aspect minimaliste mais néanmoins raffiné. Toutes les ouvertures sont conçues pour laisser entrer un maximum de lumière naturelle tout en limitant la vue de l'extérieur. Les intérieurs forment ainsi un ensemble bien équilibré entre les surfaces vitrées et les surfaces pleines. La salle de séjour au rez-de-chaussée constitue le cœur de la maison principale, avec la salle à manger. Celle-ci est reliée à la terrasse par un grand mur de verre. Un jardin caché des regards extérieurs prolonge la perspective. La maison d'hôtes, plus basse et plus dépouillée, offre le même aspect à une échelle plus réduite. Située à l'extrémité de la parcelle, cette dernière s'ouvre également sur le jardin. Les deux bâtiments sont chauffés par une pompe à chaleur à eau souterraine et leurs toits sont recouverts de verdure.

ARCHITECTS: UNTERLANDSTÄTTNER ARCHITEKTEN /// **COMPLETION:** 2018 /// **FLOOR AREA:** 400 M² AND 210 M² (4,305 FT² AND 2,260 FT²) /// **PHOTOS:** MICHAEL HEINRICH, FLORIAN HOLZHERR

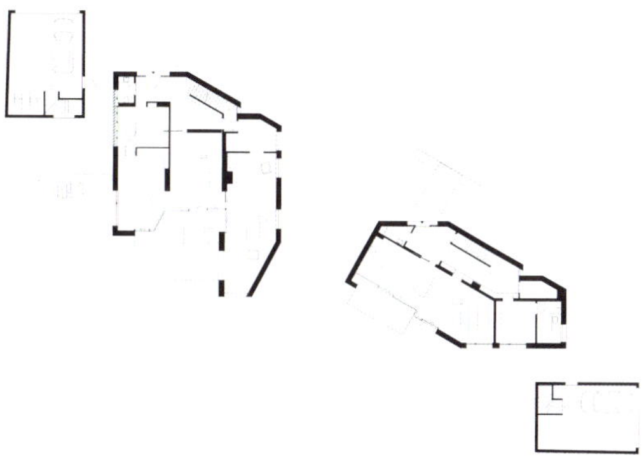

Street view

Straßenansicht

Vue de la rue

Ground floor plan

Grundrisse Erdgeschoss

Plan du rez-de-chaussée

Exterior view Außenansicht Vue extérieure

Interiors Innenräume Intérieurs

ARCHITECTS: DIETRICH | UNTERTRIFALLER ARCHITEKTEN /// **COMPLETION:** 2016 /// **FLOOR AREA:** 210 M² (2,260 FT²) /// **PHOTOS:** BRUNO KLOMFAR, ALBRECHT IMMANUEL SCHNABEL

Street façade

Fassade an der Straßenseite

Façade côté rue

Plans of three levels

Grundrisse Erdgeschoss, 1. und 2. Obergeschoss

Plan des trois étages

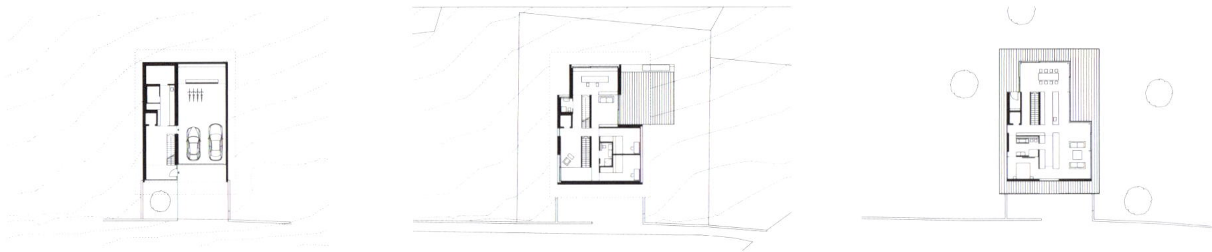

Façade opening up towards the garden

Fassade an der Gartenseite

Façade côté jardin

HOUSE D

BREGENZ, AUSTRIA

The view of Lake Constance and Bregenz just as much the hilly topography determined the design of this volume, which is simple yet with a twist. Two storeys, one of which is dug into the slope and includes the entrance and staircase leading up, are made of exposed concrete. On the top sits a wooden level dedicated to the living space. Planned as an open space, it fluidly connects the kitchen, dining space, and living room together, with a bedroom and bathroom flanked by a wardrobe room. The façades facing the garden are fully glazed to fill the whole interior with light. The space is practically free of superfluous corridors, and is extended outdoors by a spacious all-round veranda covered by a flat roof. The middle floor accommodates children's rooms and a guest room, as well as a home office. Just like the outside, the materials used inside the house are an elegant combination of concrete, wood, and glass. The façade from the street side discretely reduces the views for the occupants' privacy without creating the impression of a block wall, to harmonise with other elevations.

Der Blick auf den Bodensee und die Stadt Bregenz sowie die hügelige Topographie bestimmten die Gestaltung des Gebäudes, das zwar einfach wirkt, aber das gewisse Etwas besitzt. Die beiden unteren Geschosse, von denen eines in den Hang geschnitten ist und den Eingang und die Treppe zu diesem umfasst, bestehen aus Sichtbeton. Oben befindet sich ein aus Holz gebautes Stockwerk, in dem der Wohnbereich untergebracht ist. Als offener Raum konzipiert, umfasst er Küche, Ess- und Wohnzimmer sowie ein Schlafzimmer und ein von einem Ankleidezimmer flankiertes Bad. Die Fassaden mit Blick auf den Garten sind vollständig verglast, sodass das Haus mit Licht erfüllt ist. Der Raum ist frei von unnötigen Korridoren und wird durch eine große, von einem Flachdach überdachte Veranda nach außen hin erweitert. In der mittleren Etage befinden sich die Kinderzimmer, ein Gästezimmer und ein Büro. Wie außen sind die im Inneren des Hauses verwendeten Materialien eine elegante Kombination aus Beton, Holz und Glas. Die straßenseitige Fassade schränkt den Blick ein, um die Privatsphäre der Bewohner zu wahren, ohne den Eindruck einer Blockwand zu erwecken, und bleibt so im Einklang mit den anderen Fassaden.

La vue sur le lac de Constance et sur la ville de Brégence, tout comme la topographie vallonnée, ont déterminé la conception de cet édifice simple d'apparence mais qui n'est pas privé pour autant d'un certain cachet. Les deux étages inférieurs, dont l'un est creusé dans la pente et comprend l'entrée et l'escalier qui y mène, sont en béton apparent. Au sommet se trouve un étage en bois qui accueille les pièces d'habitation. Conçu comme un espace ouvert, il réunit la cuisine, la salle à manger et le salon ainsi qu'une chambre et une salle de bain flanquées d'un dressing. Les façades donnant sur le jardin sont entièrement vitrées pour que la lumière pénètre à l'intérieur de la maison. L'espace est exempt de couloirs superflus et se prolonge à l'extérieur par une vaste véranda périphérique recouverte d'un toit plat. L'étage intermédiaire accueille les chambres des enfants, une chambre d'amis, ainsi qu'un bureau. Tout comme à l'extérieur, les matériaux utilisés à l'intérieur de la maison sont une combinaison élégante de béton, de bois et de verre. La façade côté rue restreint discrètement la vue pour préserver l'intimité des occupants sans créer l'impression d'un mur aveugle et reste ainsi à l'unisson des autres façades.

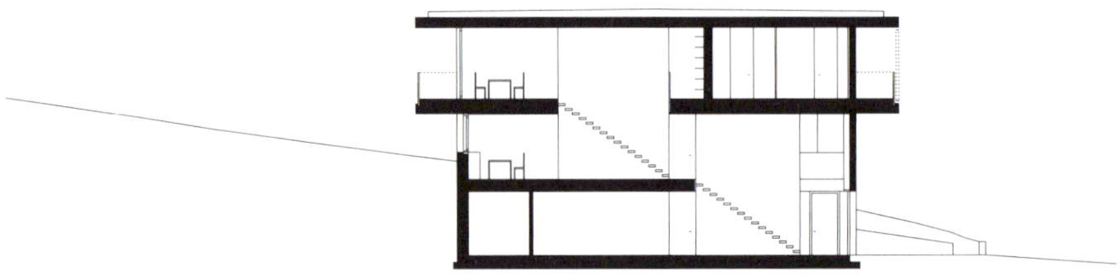

Section Schnitt Section

Interiors Innenräume Intérieurs

Interiors Innenräume Intérieurs

Entrance Eingangsbereich Entrée

ARCHITECTS: URBEN SEYBOTH ARCHITEKTEN /// **COMPLETION:** 2017 /// **FURTHER PARTICIPANTS:** LANDSCHAFTSPLANER ENEA GMBH, RAPPERWIL-JONA, SWITZERLAND /// **FLOOR AREA:** 720 M² (7,750 FT²) /// **PHOTOS:** KUSTER FREY FOTOGRAFIE

VILLA TÜFEN-GRABEN

RAPPERSWIL-JONA, SWITZERLAND

Located on Lake Zurich, this ensemble consists of the villa, a barn, and a classical garden with two pavilions and is a listed monument. The architects, asked for additional accommodation units, advised against converting existing buildings, recommending that it would be better to build a new construction on the empty space in the plot. They nevertheless used the supporting wall and two garden pavilions as the base for three pavilion-like buildings. The modern geometric forms are intentionally contrasting with the neo-classical style of the historical villa. This stark difference is neutralised by the use of a similar colour palette. The new and old coexist, near each other yet separated by areas of park-like garden. The new additions to this unusual complex, with their irregular volumes, fit into the naturally grown and inclining terrain. In particular, the top elements, which are enveloped in wooden cladding, merge with the natural context despite their large scale. Numerous significantly sized openings bring vistas of the lake inside. Interestingly, the building area is the zone of the Roman settlement "Centum Prata" and in preparation for the construction, archaeological excavations resulted in the discovery of precious ancient artefacts.

Diese am Zürichsee gelegene Residenz besteht aus einer Villa, einer Scheune und einem klassischen Garten mit zwei Pavillons. Das Gebäude steht unter Denkmalschutz. Die Architekten, die mit der Schaffung von zusätzlichem Wohnraum beauftragt wurden, rieten vom Umbau der bestehenden Gebäude ab und empfahlen stattdessen den Bau eines neuen Gebäudes auf einem noch leeren Teil des Grundstücks. Dennoch integrierten sie eine Stützmauer und die beiden Gartenpavillons in drei neue Gebäude in Form von Pavillons. Die modernen geometrischen Formen stehen in bewusstem Kontrast zum neoklassizistischen Stil der ursprünglichen Villa. Dieser Unterschied im Stil wird jedoch durch die Verwendung einer ähnlichen Farbpalette gemildert. Das Neue und das Alte koexistieren dicht beieinander und doch durch parkähnliche Gartenbereiche getrennt. Die neuen Gebäude dieses ungewöhnlichen Ensembles fügen sich mit ihren unregelmäßigen Ausmaßen in die von einem schrägen, bewachsenen Gelände geprägte Landschaft ein. Die holzvertäfelten Bauelemente des Obergeschosses verschmelzen trotz ihrer Größe mit ihrer natürlichen Umgebung. Zahlreiche große Fenster bieten einen Blick auf den See. Die Baustelle war einst der Ort der römischen Siedlung „Centum Prata". Archäologische Ausgrabungen vor dem Bau haben wertvolle antike Artefakte freigelegt.

Situé au bord du lac de Zurich, cet ensemble se compose d'une villa, d'une grange et d'un jardin classique avec deux pavillons. Il est classé monument historique. Les architectes, qui avaient reçu pour mission de bâtir un logis supplémentaire, ont déconseillé de transformer les bâtiments existants et recommandé à la place la construction d'un nouvel édifice sur un terrain encore vide. Ils ont néanmoins intégré un mur de soutènement et les deux pavillons du jardin à trois nouveaux bâtiments en forme de pavillons. Les formes géométriques modernes contrastent intentionnellement avec le style néo-classique de la villa d'origine. Cette différence de style est cependant atténuée par l'utilisation d'une palette de couleurs similaire. Le nouveau et l'ancien coexistent, proches l'un de l'autre mais séparés par le jardin dont les dimensions s'apparentent à celles d'un parc. Les nouveaux bâtiments de cet ensemble inhabituel, avec leurs volumes irréguliers, s'intègrent dans le paysage marqué par un terrain incliné et couvert de végétation. Les parties en bois au premier étage se fondent particulièrement bien dans l'environnement naturel malgré leur taille imposante. De nombreuses fenêtres de grandes dimensions offrent une vue sur le lac. À noter aussi, l'aire de construction était autrefois celle de la colonie romaine «Centum Prata». Des fouilles archéologiques menées préalablement à la construction ont mis à jour de précieux objets anciens.

Exterior view Außenansicht Vue extérieure

Terrace view

Blick auf die Terrasse

Vue sur la terrasse

Interiors Innenräume Intérieurs

VILLA TOREKOV

SKÅNE, SWEDEN

Torekov is a very popular destination for the summer holidays in Sweden. The clients commissioning Villa Torekov wanted it to be a house where they could also stay in the winter. The plot is situated on a wooded hill surrounded by open fields. To the west of the site, the house enjoys an unobstructed view of the Kattegatt Sea and the town centre of Torekov. The one-level volume is a simple, mid-century modern-style house that fits perfectly within its natural surroundings due to its light structure and transparent façade. The uncomplicated floorplan is divided into an open public area and a more intimate private one. The first part encompasses a kitchen, living area, and a dining space, which is located a few steps up. Not only does this part have an open-plan character, but it can also be extended towards the garden by windows that open up the entire room in the corners toward the generously roofed terrace. To maintain the visual continuity of the inside and outside parts, their ceilings are made of the same material. Two bedrooms with a bathroom and utility rooms are placed in the back of the villa.

Torekov ist ein beliebtes Sommerziel in Schweden. Die Bauherren der Torekov-Villa wünschten sich ein Haus, in dem sie auch im Winter wohnen können. Das Grundstück liegt auf einem bewaldeten Hügel, der von offenen Feldern umgeben ist. Im Westen hat das Haus einen atemberaubenden Blick auf das Kattegatt und das Zentrum von Torekov. Das einstöckige Gebäude ist ein einfaches, modernes Haus im mid-century Stil, , das sich dank seiner leichten Struktur und transparenten Fassade perfekt in seine natürliche Umgebung einfügt. Das Haus ist auf sehr einfache Weise in einen offenen Gemeinschaftsbereich und einen intimeren privaten Bereich unterteilt. Der erste Teil besteht aus einer Küche, einem Wohnzimmer und einem Esszimmer, das ein paar Stufen höher liegt. Dieser Teil bildet nicht nur einen offenen Raum, sondern kann durch Fenster in den Ecken, die den ganzen Raum zur überdachten Terrasse hin öffnen, auch zum Garten hin erweitert werden. Um die visuelle Kontinuität der Innen- und Außenbereiche zu erhalten, bestehen ihre Decken aus dem gleichen Material. Auf der Rückseite der Villa befinden sich zwei Schlafzimmer mit Badezimmern und Wirtschaftsräumen.

En Suède, Torekov est une destination très prisée des estivants. Les clients qui ont passé commande de la villa souhaitaient que ce soit une maison où ils puissent également séjourner en hiver. La parcelle est située sur une colline boisée entourée de champs. À l'ouest, la maison bénéficie d'une vue imprenable sur la baie du Kattegatt et le centre-ville de Torekov. Le bâtiment de plain-pied est une maison simple, moderne et fidèle au style « mid-century » qui s'intègre parfaitement dans son environnement naturel grâce à sa structure légère et à sa façade transparente. La maison est divisée de façon très simple en un espace public ouvert et un espace privé plus intime. La première partie comprend une cuisine, un salon et une salle à manger. Cette dernière est surélevée de quelques marches. Cette partie forme non seulement un espace ouvert, mais elle peut aussi être prolongée vers le jardin par des fenêtres situées dans les coins qui ouvrent toute la pièce vers la terrasse couverte. Pour maintenir la continuité visuelle des parties intérieure et extérieure, leurs plafonds sont réalisés dans le même matériau. Deux chambres à coucher avec salle de bains et pièces de service sont placées à l'arrière de la villa.

Exterior view Außenansicht Vue extérieure

ARCHITECTS: WÅHLIN ARKITEKTER /// **COMPLETION:** 2018 /// **FLOOR AREA:** 100 M² (1,076 FT²) /// **PHOTOS:** OLA ÖSTERLING

Living and dining area

Wohn- und Esszimmer

Salon et salle à manger

Terrace view

Blick auf die Terrasse

Vue sur la terrasse

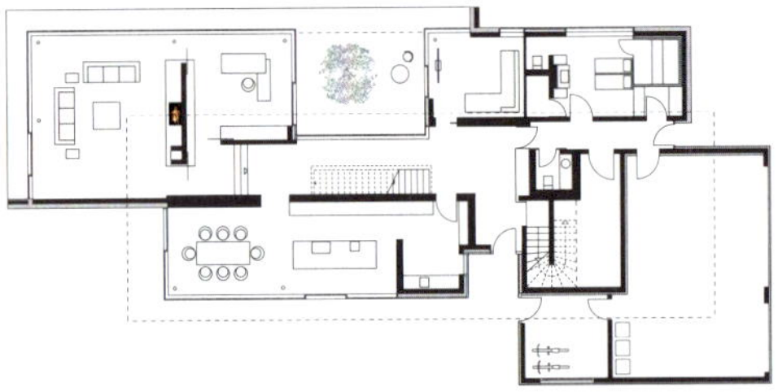

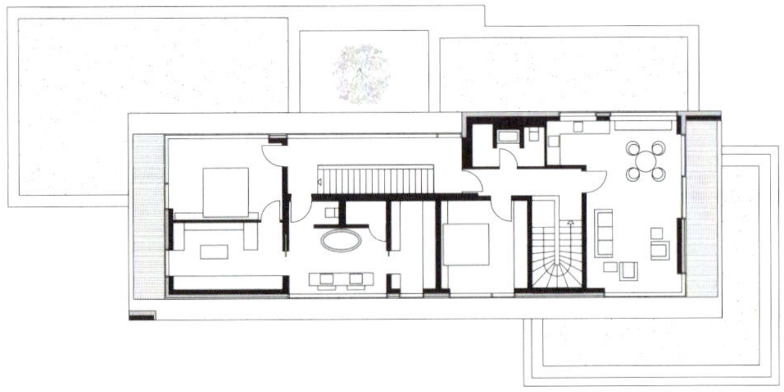

ARCHITECTS: WEBER + HUMMEL ARCHITEKTEN /// **COMPLETION:** 2018 /// **FLOOR AREA:** 440 M^2 (4,736 FT^2) ///
PHOTOS: ROLAND HALBE

VILLA IN FRANKEN

FRANKEN, GERMANY

This sophisticated composition of geometric volumes sits lightly on its sloping, elongated plot. A flowing continuum of spaces is at the heart of this design, both within the building and in relation to the landscape. The changing panoramic views of the Main River valley form an integral part of the interiors thanks to significantly glazed walls. The walls are not supposed to separate the spaces from the surroundings but to put both in dialogue with nature. The villa is constructed of two interlocking volumes on three levels, adjusted to the terrain's topography. The horizontal construction offers extensive floor space and numerous outdoor terraces. A private garden on the south side is protected from views for privacy and conveniently serves as an extension of the dining area and the kitchen. The upper floors are dedicated to the bedrooms and also have spacious terraces offering distant views. The building's high-quality materials, precision in details, and aesthetic minimalism have resulted in a very pure and elegant look, which is enhanced by the timeless combination of white walls, glass, and wooden elements. Filled with light, the villa offers comfortable and well-planned everyday life spaces.

Nicht der kubisch geschlossene Baukörper mit seinen rigiden Trennungen, sondern das Raumkontinuum mit fließenden Übergängen sowie die Behandlung des Außenraums als integraler Bestandteil und Bühnenbild der Architektur, stellten wesentliche Gestaltungsparameter für die Villa in Franken dar. Eine besondere Herausforderung war dabei das langgestreckte Grundstück, das mit dem Potential eines beeindruckenden Panoramablicks ins nördlich gelegene Maintal ausgestattet, gleichzeitig aber auch mit der „Hypothek" einer südlich gelegenen Erschließungsstraße belastet war. Die gestalterische Umsetzung besteht aus zwei ineinander verschränkten Baukörpern, die sich über drei Wohnniveaus dem Geländeverlauf anpassen und zum Fernblick öffnen. Gleichzeitig entstehen durch den Gebäudeversatz ein nach zwei Seiten offenes Atrium sowie ein sichtgeschützter privater Südgarten, an den der Essbereich mit Küche anschließt. Die im Obergeschoss liegenden Schlafräume sind mit großzügigen Terrassen ausgestattet und genießen Privatheit und Fernblick gleichermaßen. Die Atmosphäre der Innenräume ist geprägt durch ästhetisch motivierte Reduktion, präzise Details und wertige Materialien. Geölter Eichdielenboden wechselt sich mit fein gebürsteten Kalksandsteinplatten ab, während die weiß-matten Oberflächen von Wänden und sämtlichen Einbauten einen ruhigen Hintergrund bilden. In Verbindung mit architekturintegriertem Licht und wechselnden Ausblicken in die Landschaft sind so Raumbereiche mit unverwechselbarem Charakter entstanden, die nicht getrennt, sondern im Dialog mit der Natur stehen.

Cette demeure aux formes géométriques épurées est construite sur un terrain allongé et incliné. Elle a été conçue comme une enchaînement harmonieux d'espaces imbriqués qui se fondent dans le paysage. Grâce à des murs largement vitrés, le panorama splendide qu'offre la vallée du Main fait partie intégrante des intérieurs. Les murs ne sont pas censés séparer les espaces de l'environnement mais bien initier un dialogue avec la nature. La villa est construite en deux blocs emboîtés l'un dans l'autre sur trois étages et adaptés à la topographie du terrain. Sa configuration horizontale assure une grande surface au sol et permet d'avoir de nombreuses terrasses extérieures. Un jardin privé situé sur le côté sud est protégé des regards pour plus d'intimité et sert commodément de prolongement de la salle à manger et de la cuisine. Les étages supérieurs sont réservés aux appartements privés et disposent également de grandes terrasses avec une vue imprenable sur les alentours. Les matériaux de haute qualité, la minutie dans les détails et le minimalisme esthétique du bâtiment ont contribué à son aspect très pur et élégant mis en avant par la juxtaposition classique de murs blancs, de verre et d'éléments en bois. Baignée de lumière, la villa offre des pièces confortables et bien aménagées.

Floor plans Grundrisse Plan des étages

Exterior view Außenansicht Vue extérieure

Exterior view Außenansicht Vue extérieure

Interiors Innenräume Intérieurs

ARCHITECTS: WOODS BAGOT /// **COMPLETION:** 2018 /// **FURTHER PARTICIPANTS:** WOODS BAGOT - NIK KARALIS, LAWRENCE NG (ARCHITECTURE), HECKER GUTHRIE – PAUL HECKER, JOSH WATT AND WOODS BAGOT – SARAH ALESSI, MELISSA BLANDFORD (INTERIORS), SIMONE HAAG (FURNITURE, STYLING) /// **FLOOR AREA:** 880 M^2 (9,472 FT^2) /// **PHOTOS:** TREVOR MEIN

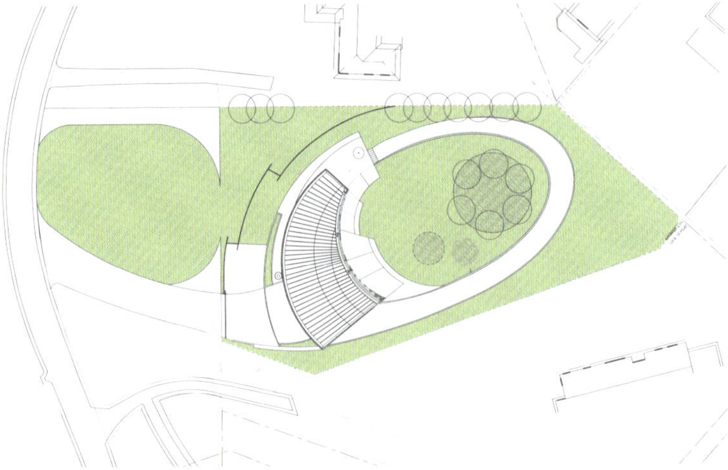

Exterior view Außenansicht Vue extérieure

Site plan Lageplan Plan du site

TIDAL ARC HOUSE

FLINDERS, VICTORIA, AUSTRALIA

The original shape of Tidal Arc House is the architects' inventive response to the majestic Australian coastal landscape. Located on the cliff edge of a peninsula town, the house's distinctive curved form echoes the massive water movement of the Southern Ocean. The dynamic geometry mimics the unpredictable character of the weather changes and tidal movements. In parallel, the interiors, organised on three levels, also employ sinuous twists and rhythms. The zoning was planned according to the outward vistas and the movements of the sun, moon, and tide. Hugging the edge of the oval plot on the coastline side, it opens to the seascape through a series of regularly placed windows, while on the other side is an intimate garden. The exact location was defined not only by the topographic specifics but also by the complexity of its adjoining neighbours. Responding to the landscape and connecting the inhabitants to nature were the architects' main goals. The architects used concrete and limestone for the exterior and charcoal timber, ash grey marble, and brass for the interiors, materials that form a protective shell against the strong Australian sunshine.

Die besondere Form des Tidal Arc Hauses ist eine originelle Hommage der Architekten an die herrliche Küstenlandschaft, die es überblickt. Das am Rande einer Klippe gelegene Haus in einer Halbinsel-Stadt erinnert in seiner markanten Krümmung an die Bewegung der Gewässer des Südlichen Ozeans. Die dynamische Geometrie ahmt die Unvorhersehbarkeit von Wetteränderungen und Gezeitenbewegungen nach. Auch die Innenräume, die sich auf drei Stockwerke verteilen, weisen Mäander und geschwungene Formen auf. Die Einteilung basierte auf dem Panorama und den Bewegungen von Sonne, Mond und Gezeiten. Auf der Küstenseite folgt die Architektur dem Oval des Geländes, und die Fassade öffnet sich durch eine Reihe von regelmäßig angeordneten Fenstern zum Meer hin, während sich auf der anderen Seite ein privater Garten befindet. Der genaue Grundriss der Villa wurde nicht nur durch die topographischen Gegebenheiten, sondern auch durch die Anwesenheit von Nachbarhäusern bestimmt. Die Architekten richteten ihr Hauptaugenmerk darauf, das Haus mit der Landschaft in Einklang zu bringen und seine Bewohner mit der Natur zu verbinden. Sie verwendeten Beton und Kalkstein für den Außenbereich und anthrazitfarbenes Holz, aschgrauen Marmor und Messing für den Innenbereich. Diese Materialien bilden eine Schutzschicht gegen die starke australische Sonne.

La forme particulière de la Tidal Arc House est un hommage des architectes au magnifique paysage côtier qu'elle surplombe. L'arrondi distinctif de la maison, située au bord d'une falaise dans une ville péninsulaire, fait écho au mouvement des eaux de l'Océan Austral. La géométrie dynamique imite le caractère imprévisible des changements de temps et du mouvement de marées. De même, on retrouve dans les intérieurs, répartis sur trois étages, des méandres et des formes sinueuses. Le découpage a été établi en fonction du panorama et des mouvements du soleil, de la lune et des marées. Côté littoral, l'architecture suit l'ovale du terrain et la façade s'ouvre sur le paysage marin par une série de fenêtres régulièrement placées, tandis que de l'autre côté se trouve un jardin privé. La disposition exacte de la villa a été dictée non seulement par des spécificités topographiques, mais aussi par la présence des maisons avoisinantes. Les architectes s'étaient donné pour but de mettre en valeur le paysage et rapprocher les habitants de la nature. Ils ont utilisé du béton et de la pierre calcaire pour l'extérieur et du bois anthracite, du marbre gris cendré et du laiton pour l'intérieur. Ces matériaux forment une enveloppe protectrice contre la force du soleil particulièrement vive en Australie.

Interiors Innenräume Intérieurs

WOHNHAUS F9

STUTTGART, GERMANY

The small plot in a dense residential environment required an inventive solution to create a comfortable and highly functional house for a family of five. This monolithic volume is curiously penetrated by numerous corner and side openings. In addition to letting in light from various angles and offering views, these also give the pure form a distinctive character. As is the outer shell, the inside of the house is also quite homogenous. The materials used in this project are reduced to wood and concrete, which remain entirely visible on the walls, floor, and ceiling to enhance the minimalist effect. The interiors are planned well to fit numerous functions into the relatively small floor area – the kitchen and living spaces are on the ground level, children's rooms on the first floor, and the parents' quarters and common gallery space are on the top floor, with an original slanting roof. Interestingly, all pipes were laid directly into the concrete, like the floor heating that contributes to the material's temperature control (cool in the summer and warm in the winter). To make this stylish house sustainable as well, it is heated by a heat pump with a storage tank located under the building.

Um auf diesem kleinen Grundstück in einem dichten Wohngebiet ein komfortables und funktionelles Haus für eine fünfköpfige Familie zu bauen, mussten die Architekten eine innovative Lösung finden: Das monolithische Gebäude, das sie sich vorstellten, hat erstaunlich viele Eck- und Seitenfenster. Diese verleihen den schlichten Formen des Gebäudes eine unverwechselbare Note und lassen natürliches Licht herein, während sie gleichzeitig eine schöne Aussicht auf die Umgebung bieten. Wie bei der Außenhülle ist auch das Innere des Hauses sehr homogen. Die verwendeten Materialien sind auf Holz und Beton reduziert, die an den Wänden, dem Boden und der Decke voll sichtbar bleiben, um den minimalistischen Effekt zu verstärken. Die Innenräume sind so gestaltet, dass mehrere Räume auf einer begrenzten Grundfläche untergebracht werden können - die Küche und die Wohnräume befinden sich im Erdgeschoss, die Kinderzimmer im ersten Stock, die Elternzimmer und die gemeinsame Galerie im Obergeschoss unter einem ursprünglichen Schrägdach. Bemerkenswert ist auch die Tatsache, dass alle Rohre direkt in den Beton verlegt wurden, wie zum Beispiel die Fußbodenheizung, die dazu beiträgt, die Temperatur des Materials zu kontrollieren (kühl im Sommer und warm im Winter). Dieses elegante Haus wird durch eine Wärmepumpe mit einem unter dem Gebäude befindlichen Speicher beheizt.

Pour construire une maison confortable et fonctionnelle destinée à une famille de cinq personnes sur ce petit terrain situé dans un quartier résidentiel dense, les architectes ont dû trouver une solution innovante : Le bâtiment monolithique qu'ils ont imaginé est ainsi traversé de nombreuses fenêtres d'angles et latérales. Celles-ci donnent une touche distinctive aux formes épurées de la construction et laissent passer la lumière naturelle à l'intérieur tout en offrant une belle vue sur les environs. Tout comme l'enveloppe extérieure, l'intérieur de la maison est très homogène. Les matériaux utilisés se réduisent au bois et au béton qui restent entièrement visibles sur les murs, le sol et le plafond pour renforcer l'effet minimaliste. Les intérieurs sont conçus pour accueillir de nombreuses pièces dans une surface au sol limitée - la cuisine et les pièces de séjour sont au rez-de-chaussée, les chambres d'enfants au premier étage, celles des parents et la galerie commune au dernier étage sous un toit à l'inclinaison insolite. À noter également ; tous les tuyaux ont été installés directement dans le béton, comme le chauffage par le sol qui contribue au contrôle de la température du matériau (frais en été et chaud en hiver). Cette maison élégante est chauffée par une pompe à chaleur avec un réservoir de stockage situé sous le bâtiment.

ARCHITECTS: ZOLL ARCHITEKTEN STADTPLANER /// **COMPLETION:** 2016 /// **FLOOR AREA:** 215 M² (2,314 FT²) /// **PHOTOS:** ZOOEY BRAUN FOTOGRAFIE

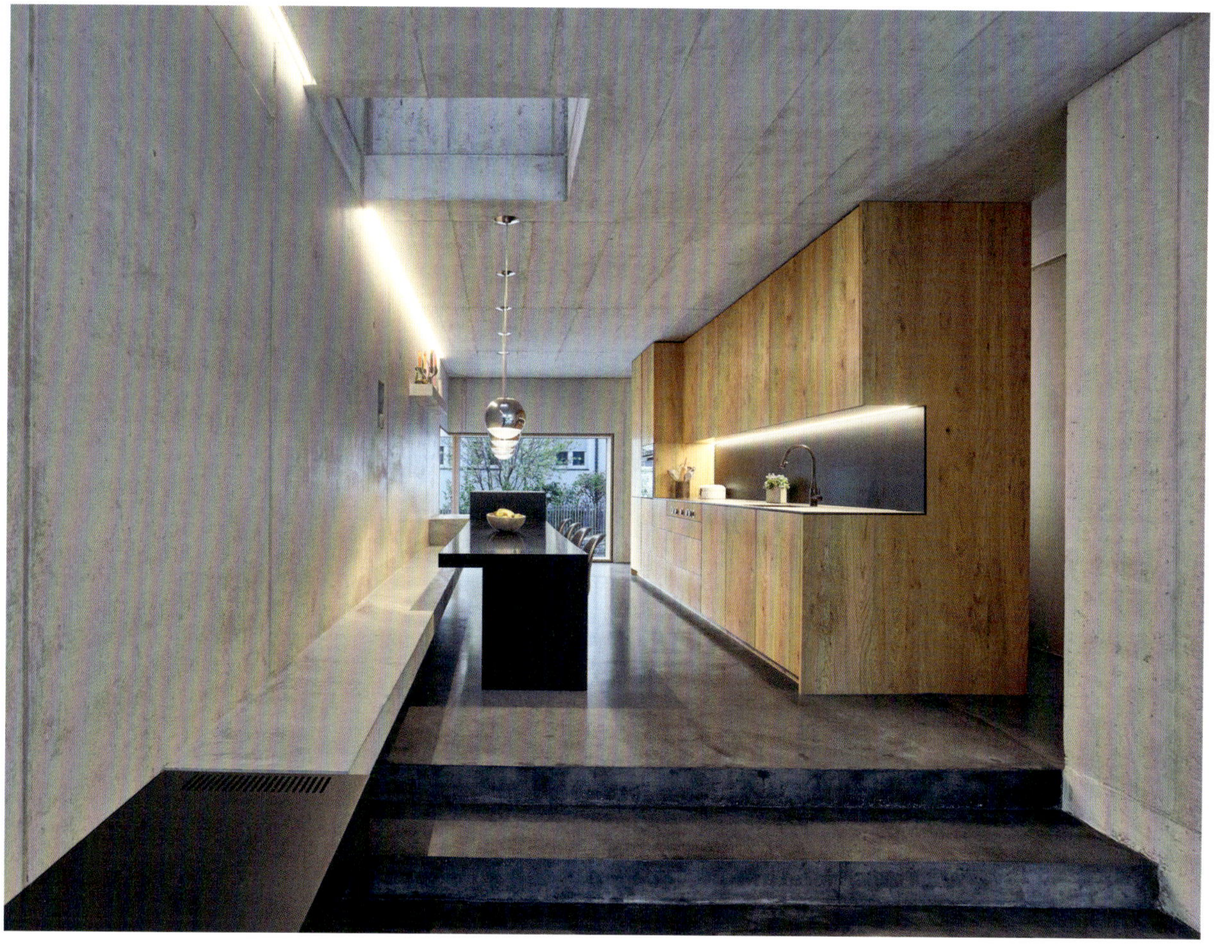

Interiors Innenräume Intérieurs

Façade opening up towards the garden

Fassade an der Gartenseite

Façade côté jardin

Street view

Straßenansicht

Vue de la rue

WOHNHAUS K6

KLOSTERNEUBURG, AUSTRIA

The setting for this complex and dynamic house for a family with two children is a very steep hillside located in a town just outside of Vienna. While the impressive residence sits on top of the hill, the underground garage is accessible through a long-covered driveway. Constructed in reinforced concrete in combination with steel columns, the volume is based on the multiplication of the triangle form. Inside, the spatial arrangement was planned according to the topography and the way the sun travels, particularly with summer warmth in consideration. The top level, with a white smooth plaster façade and spectacular views, has a spacious terrace and an infinity pool that fluidly extends the open residential area, which includes the master bedroom with a dressing room, bathroom, and sauna, as well as the children's rooms. A sculptural spiral staircase connects this private part with the living and dining areas and a kitchen on the ground floor. The main entrance is located in the basement and can be reached from the lower garden level or from the garage. This floor also includes a wardrobe area and a study, as well as a guest room with an en-suite bathroom.

Ein steiler Hügel am Stadtrand von Wien ist die Kulisse für dieses elegante und dynamische Haus, das eine Familie mit zwei Kindern beherbergt. Die imposante Residenz befindet sich an der höchsten Erhebung des Hügels. Die Tiefgarage ist über eine lange überdachte Zufahrt erreichbar. Das aus Stahlbeton in Kombination mit Stahlstützen errichtete Gebäude ist als Nebeneinander von Dreiecken konzipiert. Die Topografie und der Lauf der Sonne, die im Sommer die Innenräume erwärmt, prägten die Raumaufteilung. Das Obergeschoss mit seiner glatten weißen Putzfassade und spektakulären Panoramaaussichten verfügt über eine geräumige Terrasse und einen Infinity-Pool, der sich nahtlos in den offenen Innenraum mit dem Hauptschlafzimmer mit Ankleideraum, Bad und Sauna sowie den Kinderschlafzimmern fortsetzt. Eine Wendeltreppe mit skulpturalen Formen verbindet diesen privaten Bereich mit dem Wohn- und Esszimmer sowie mit der Küche im Erdgeschoss. Der Haupteingang befindet sich im Untergeschoss. Von außen ist er vom Gartengeschoss oder von der Garage aus zugänglich. Im unteren Stockwerk befinden sich außerdem ein Schrankzimmer und ein Büro sowie ein Gästezimmer mit angrenzendem Bad.

Une colline très escarpée située dans les faubourgs de Vienne est le cadre naturel de cette maison aussi sophistiquée que dynamique qui abrite une famille avec deux enfants. Cette résidence imposante se trouve au sommet de la colline. Le garage souterrain est accessible par une longue allée couverte. Construit en béton armé combiné avec des colonnes en acier, le bâtiment est conçu comme une juxtaposition de triangles. À l'intérieur, l'aménagement de l'espace a été pensé en tenant compte de la topographie et de la façon dont le soleil se déplace et réchauffe les intérieurs durant l'été. L'étage supérieur, avec sa façade en plâtre blanc lisse et sa vue panoramique spectaculaire, dispose d'une terrasse spacieuse et d'une piscine à débordement qui prolonge de manière fluide l'espace intérieur ouvert comprenant la chambre principale avec un dressing, une salle de bain et un sauna, ainsi que les chambres des enfants. Un escalier en colimaçon aux formes sculpturales relie cette partie privée au salon et à la salle à manger ainsi qu'à la cuisine du rez-de-chaussée. L'entrée principale se trouve au sous-sol. De l'extérieur, elle est accessible depuis le rez-de-jardin ou depuis le garage. L'étage inférieur inclut aussi un espace garde-robe et un bureau, ainsi qu'une chambre d'amis avec une salle de bain attenante.

Exterior view Außenansicht Vue extérieure

ARCHITECTS: A01 ARCHITECTS /// **COMPLETION:** 2017 /// **FURTHER PARTICIPANTS:** TRINKL (STONEMASON), UNTERLEUTHNER (CARPENTRY, JOINERY), WOSCHITZ ENGINEERING (STRUCTURAL ENGINEERING) /// **FLOOR AREA:** 325 M² (3,498 FT²) /// **PHOTOS:** NADINE BLANCHARD

Terrace view

Blick auf die Terrasse

Vue sur la terrasse

Interiors Innenräume Intérieurs

Living room Wohnzimmer Salon

2 HOUSES IN 1

MONTREUX, SWITZERLAND

This plot in the centre of Montreux with a great view overlooking Geneva Lake was challenging due to the highly inclined terrain and small size. The architects, however, envisioned an original four-storey volume built on a base containing the garage. The initial project included a building with two apartments placed one on top of the other, but the idea was to balance the qualities of both and provide them with equally nice views – hence the irregular and multifaceted shape, which changes the light, space, and its relationship with the surroundings on each level. From the west, the house has a monolithic appearance and seems to emerge from the ground. From the east, in contrast, it seems to be divided into two volumes. The living spaces are organised around the central staircase (there is also an internal elevator from the garage level). Two lower levels are dedicated to bedrooms, while the upper floors house living areas and the kitchen, to allow inhabitants to enjoy the best views. The use of concrete and the massive openings emphasise the solid character of the volume, while the green cover on the roof integrates the structure visually with the plot.

Dieses Grundstück im Zentrum von Montreux mit seiner atemberaubenden Aussicht auf den Genfer See war aufgrund des sehr abschüssigen Geländes und seiner geringen Größe eine echte Herausforderung für die Architekten. Sie passten ihren Entwurf den topografischen Gegebenheiten an, in dem sie ein außergewöhnliches vierstöckiges Gebäude auf einem Sockel errichteten, dessen unterstes Geschoss eine Garage birgt. Das ursprüngliche Projekt bestand aus einem Gebäude mit zwei übereinander liegenden Wohnungen, aber die Idee war, die Vorteile beider Wohnungen auszubalancieren und ihnen gleich schöne Aussichten zu bieten. Aus diesem Grund ist das Haus so unregelmäßig und abwechslungsreich gestaltet, dass sich das Zusammenspiel von Licht, Raum und die Wechselbeziehung mit der Umgebung auf jeder Ebene verändert. Im Westen hat das Haus ein monolithisches Aussehen und scheint aus dem Boden zu ragen. Im Osten hingegen scheint es in zwei Teile geteilt zu sein. Die Wohnräume sind um ein zentrales Treppenhaus herum organisiert (ein interner Aufzug ermöglicht auch die Fahrt von der Garage in die oberen Stockwerke). Die beiden unteren Stockwerke dienen als Schlafzimmer, während die beiden oberen Stockwerke das Wohnzimmer und die Küche beherbergen, um den Bewohnern die beste Aussicht auf den See zu ermöglichen. Die Verwendung von Beton und die quadratischen Fenster unterstreichen den kompakten Charakter des Gebäudes, während das bepflanzte Dach die Konstruktion in die bewaldete Umgebung integriert.

Ce terrain au centre de Montreux, avec sa vue imprenable sur le lac Léman, était un véritable défi pour les architectes en raison de sa forte inclinaison et de sa petite taille. Les architectes ont donc imaginé cet édifice original de quatre étages construit sur un socle qui abrite le garage. Le projet initial prévoyait un immeuble avec deux appartements superposés, mais l'idée était d'équilibrer les qualités des deux et de leur offrir des vues tout aussi agréables. La forme irrégulière de la construction et les multiples facettes qui modifient la lumière et l'espace à chaque étage ont été pensées dans ce sens. À l'ouest, la maison a un aspect monolithique et semble émerger du sol. À l'est, en revanche, elle a l'air d'être divisée en deux parties. Les pièces d'habitation sont organisées autour d' un escalier central (Un ascenseur intérieur permet également de circuler du garage vers les étages supérieurs). Les deux étages inférieurs servent de chambres à coucher tandis que les deux étages supérieurs abritent le séjour et la cuisine pour permettre aux habitants de profiter de la plus belle vue sur le lac. L'utilisation du béton et les fenêtres carrées soulignent le caractère compact de l'édifice tandis que le toit planté de végétation intègre la construction dans son environnement boisé.

ARCHITECTS: SBSA | SANDRI BARBARA SMANIOTTO ANDREA ARCHITETTI ASSOCIATI /// **COMPLETION:** 2016 /// **FURTHER PARTICIPANTS:** PETIGNAT & CORDOBA (ENGINEERING), SULMONI ROMONT SA (CONSTRUCTION) /// **FLOOR AREA:** 200 M² (2,153 FT²) /// **PHOTOS:** RENATO GIANTURCO

General view Gesamtansicht Vue générale

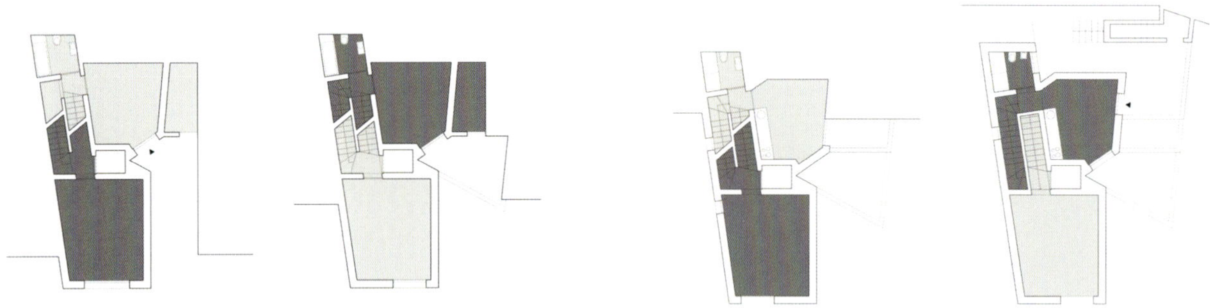

Plans of all levels

Grundrisse aller Geschosse

Plan des étages

Exterior view Außenansicht Vue extérieure

Interiors Innenräume Intérieurs

INDEX

HPA + ARCHITEKTUR (158 – 161)
www.hpa.de

INDEX ARCHITECTES SÀRL (166 – 169)
www.index-arch.ch

ROBERT KONIECZNY – KWK PROMES (162 – 165)
www.kwkpromes.pl

LIEBEL/ARCHITEKTEN BDA (170 – 173)
www.liebelarchitekten.de

MECANOO (14 – 19)
www.mecanoo.nl

MOKE ARCHITECTEN GIANNI CITO (174 – 177)
www.mokearchitecten.nl

NAT OFFICE - CHRISTIAN GASPARINI ARCHITECT (178 – 181)
www.natoffice.it

NICOLA PROBST ARCHITETTI (186 – 189)
www.nicolaprobst.com

NOARQ - JOSÉ CARLOS NUNES DE OLIVEIRA (182 – 185)
www.noarq.com

OLIVER CHRISTEN ARCHITEKTEN (196 – 199)
www.oliverchristen.ch

PHILIPPARCHITEKTEN ANNA PHILIPP (200 – 205)
www.philipparchitekten.de

PIETRIARCHITECTES (212 – 215)
www.pietriarchitectes.com

QUERKOPF ARCHITEKTEN (206 – 211)
www.querkopf-architekten.de

REACT ARCHITECTS (216 – 221)
www.re-act.gr

REM'A (222 – 225)
www.rem-a.com

ROB DUBOIS ARQUITECTE (226 – 231)
www.rob-dubois.com

SBSA (298 – 301)
www.sbsa.it

SCHAMP & SCHMALÖER ARCHITEKTEN STADTPLANER PARTGMBB (246 – 249)
www.schamp-schmaloeer.de

SCHILLER ARCHITEKTUR BDA (232 – 235)
www.schiller-architektur.de

SODAA (236 – 239)
www.sodaa.eu

SUPER FUTURE GROUP / ARCH. DI ROBERT LAMPRECHT (240 – 245)
www.superfuturegroup.com

TETRO ARQUITETURA (250 – 255)
www.tetro.com.br

TIAGO DO VALE ARCHITECTS (256 – 259)
www.tiagodovale.com

UNTERLANDSTÄTTNER ARCHITEKTEN (260 – 263)
www.u-architekten.de

DIETRICH | UNTERTRIFALLER ARCHITEKTEN (264 – 267)
www.dietrich.untertrifaller.com

URBEN SEYBOTH ARCHITEKTEN (270 – 273)
www.urbenseyboth.ch

VISIOARQ - ARCHITECTS (20 – 25)
www.visioarq.pt

WÅHLIN ARKITEKTER (274 – 277)
www.wahlinarkitekter.se

WEBER + HUMMEL ARCHITEKTEN (278 – 281)
www.weber-hummel.de

WOODS BAGOT (282 – 287)
www.woodsbagot.com

ZOLL ARCHITEKTEN STADPLANER (288 – 291)
www.zoll-architekten.de

The Deutsche Nationalbibliothek lists this publication in the Deutsche Nationalbibliografie; detailed bibliographic data are available on the Internet at http://dnb.dnb.de

ISBN 978-3-03768-263-0

www.braun-publishing.ch

1st edition 2020

Text, translation and layout: Agata & Pierre Toromanoff / Fancy Books Packaging (except from German text on page 279)
Copy-editing: Allison Silver Adelman (English), Maren Harting (German), Pierre Toromanoff (French)
Graphic concept: Michaela Prinz
Reproduction: Bild1Druck GmbH, Berlin

Front cover: Península House, Bernardes Arquitetura, photo by Fernando Guerra
Back cover top: Haus am Albtrauf, Henrik Isermann – Hi Architektur, photo by Jürgen Pollak; bottom: Gafarim House, Tiago Do Vale Architects, photo by João Morgado